FACE THE MOUNTAIN

*Discovering Resilience and the
Power to Change the World*

Advanced Praise for FACE THE MOUNTAIN

"*FACE THE MOUNTAIN* offers a powerful roadmap for navigating life's toughest terrains. The 3Cs of Resilience and the Five Levels of Belief provide a practical guide that truly sets this book apart. If you're ready to climb higher and believe bigger, start right here."

— **Mark Batterson**
NYT bestselling author of *The Circle Maker*

"*FACE THE MOUNTAIN* provides an insider's perspective on resilience. The author shares his own life-altering experience as well as compelling glimpses into the lives of others who triumphed against enormous odds. This book is an invaluable resource to help you summon the courage, faith, and grit to persevere."

— **Dr Gloria J. Burgess**
Author of *Pass It On!* and
Dare to Wear Your Soul on the Outside

"We all face metaphorical mountains every day and resilience is essential to personal and professional success. *FACE THE MOUNTAIN* gives you ways to build and use resilience to prevail. The author is a seasoned leader who writes from experience and that is important. I especially like the scriptural basis that is the foundation of what he teaches."

— **Mark Sanborn**
Award Winning Speaker
NYT bestselling author of *The Fred Factor*

"*FACE THE MOUNTAIN* is a powerful read that speaks directly to the heart. In this book, Paul tackles the vital pairing of faith and grit in a way that resonates with anyone striving to overcome life's obstacles. His stories hit home, offering a mix of raw honesty and practical wisdom. *FACE THE MOUNTAIN* isn't just another book on resilience—it's a guide for living out our faith when things get tough, showing how true strength comes from pressing on, even when we're up against the hardest climbs."

— **Jason Romano**
Author of *Live to Forgive* and *The Uniform of Leadership*
Sports Spectrum Host

"In FACE THE MOUNTAIN, Paul Gustavson weaves together the power of faith, grit, and the Theory of Resiliency, providing a practical and inspiring guide to overcoming adversity. By the end of this book, you'll be ready to face any mountain with newfound strength and clarity."

— **Mark Cole**
Owner/CEO *Maxwell Leadership*

"Resilience, to me, is a choice we all can make. I've dedicated my life to it. In FACE THE MOUNTAIN, Paul Gustavson captures this essence beautifully, exploring what it truly means to face life's challenges with courage, competence, and compassion. His insights resonate deeply with my belief that resilience is not just about bouncing back but about bouncing forward and growing stronger through every struggle. This book is a roadmap for anyone ready to confront their mountains and discover their power to move forward. It is an inspiring and essential read for those determined to change their world."

— **Bonnie St. John**
Paralympic Medalist and
Author of *Micro-Resilience*

"FACE THE MOUNTAIN is a call to live with resilience, built on faith and grit. Paul dives deep into the 3Cs of Resilience—Competence, Courage, and Compassion—showing how these traits equip us to overcome any obstacle. His stories cut through the noise, reminding us that we're meant to face the hard stuff head-on, trusting that God has our back. If you're ready to step up, embrace the climb, and build the kind of resilience that matters, this book is for you."

— **David and Jason Benham**
entrepreneurs and best-selling authors of
Whatever The Cost and *Expert Ownership*

"Paul Gustavson's FACE THE MOUNTAIN is a masterful exploration of how faith and grit, combined with the ABCs of Competence, Courage, and Compassion, can help you overcome even the most daunting challenges. This book is a beacon of hope and strength."

— **Chris Robinson**
Executive VP *Maxwell Leadership*

BY PAUL GUSTAVSON

*IMAGINE: The Surprising Truth About Hope and
the 12 Powerful Ways to Invent the Future*

*BREAKING AVERAGE: The Seven Critical Factors to
Team Strong Leadership*

*SPEECH BLUEPRINT: Using Simon Sinek's TED Talk
as a Model to "Inspire Action"*

*LEADERS PRESS ON:
Discovering the Power of Perseverance*

FACE THE MOUNTAIN

Discovering Resilience and the
Power to Change the World

PAUL GUSTAVSON

Lead Edge
PRESS

LEAD EDGE PRESS
c/o Paul Gustavson

43 Town and Country Drive, Suite 129
Box #112
Fredericksburg, Virginia 22405

Copy editor: Kari Ann Hawthorne
Content editor: Daniel Hammond
Quality check: Joe Dutkiewicz

Published in the United States by Lead Edge Press

979-8-9889140-1-3 (Hardback)
979-8-9889140-0-6 (Softback)
979-8-9889140-2-0 (Kindle)
979-8-9889140-3-7 (ePub)
979-8-9889140-4-4 (Audio)

First Release: March 25, 2025

http://FaceTheMtn.com/

Epigraph

*"Great things are done
when men and mountains meet."*
– William Blake

DEDICATION

This book is dedicated to the three people in my life who may have influenced me the most:

To my mom and dad, who demonstrated the value of faith, and

To my wife, Barbara, whose unwavering grit continues to inspire me.

The world is better because of you!

Contents

Author's Note   1
1 – Landslide   3
2 – Life in Three Acts   7

ACT ONE – Competence   15
3 – Anticipate the Storms   17
4 – Build on Belief   31
5 – Commit to Duty   47

ACT TWO – Courage   61
6 – Ask, *"Why Not?"*   *63*
7 – Become Curious   77
8 – Create Calm   91

ACT THREE – Compassion   103
9 – Acclimate   105
10 – Be Intentional   119
11 – Cultivate Care   131
12 – Do It Anyway   143

Epilogue – Speak to the Mountain   159
Acknowledgments   167
Appendix A – The Climber's Prayer   169
Appendix B – The Five Mountains   171
Appendix C – The Resilience Checklist   175
About the Author   177
Endnotes   179

At Maxwell Leadership, we believe that leadership is about making a difference through values-based influence. That's why we are honored to partner with Paul Gustavson—a leader who exemplifies what it means to serve others and create lasting impact. As a part of the Maxwell Leadership Certified Team, Paul is committed to living out our mission: to equip and empower others to lead with integrity, purpose, and passion. We're in the business of adding value to people, and Paul Gustavson is a shining example of that mission in action.

AUTHOR'S NOTE

I magination will either lift you or limit you. It's an inside-out engine that propels you forward—or holds you back. But what happens when external challenges throw a wrench into that engine? How do you get back up and keep moving?

My last book, *IMAGINE*, was one I had longed to write. But this book might be the one I was called to write. What started as leftover stories and research I didn't use—*the throwaways*—came back to life to support something even more powerful than imagination: *RESILIENCE.*

After I wrote *IMAGINE*, I faced a series of challenges that left me drained. Fortunately, I recognized the tug-of-war in my mind. For nearly every limit on my imagination, I was able to catch myself—but it still left me wiped out. It required another gear beyond imagination.

Imagination gives us the spark to start, but resilience is the mechanism that keeps us in gear, moving forward through obstacles, setbacks, and unexpected challenges. That's what I needed.

As I combed through my research, I uncovered core building blocks that help us persevere and stay resilient—especially when outside forces take us off track. I began to see what was required. As I pulled the pieces together, it shaped into a guide that I needed—and maybe others do, too. That became this book.

We all face mountains—whether in business, personal endeavors, or caring for someone else. Often, these obstacles seem insurmountable. However, within each of us, we have the ability to climb them.

It takes imagination to dream, faith to believe, and grit to persevere. This book offers a guide for that journey, and I can't wait to share it with you.

Paul

1

1 — LANDSLIDE

I could taste the dirt in my mouth as I clung to the mountain. The pitch was steep, perhaps 45 degrees or more, and my fingers desperately gripped the loose dirt and rocks. With each movement, the soil beneath me threatened to give way. Doubt and fear consumed me. It was one of those moments that made me question the decisions that led me there. I wondered if I'd find a way down.

Earlier that day, my climbing partner and I had set out to conquer The Hook, a rugged peak nestled amidst the towering summits of Mount Princeton in beautiful Colorado. Standing just under 13,000 feet, The Hook may be one of the shorter Princeton peaks, but its challenge is undeniable.

Our goal seemed straightforward: reach the summit and make it back by lunch. But now, hours later, clinging precariously and separated from my partner, the mission felt anything but simple.

The climb had started well, with the crisp morning air urging us onward. As we ascended, we came across the scree field that I would get trapped on hours later. A scree field is a sloping expanse of loose rock, sometimes found on the side of a mountain, resulting from weather and erosion.

Early that morning, the scree field seemed the right path compared to the steeper outcrops of rocks and pines bordering it to the left and right. The coolness of the morning kept the stones in place, and we traversed up without any problem.

After ascending the scree field, my partner and I entered even more technical terrain. However, we had the handholds of bigger rocks and some smaller trees to grab onto. Due to the danger of climbing behind someone else, we chose to climb along two different tracks so that we wouldn't kick dirt and rocks at each other. My partner's path ended up being faster, and he reached the summit before me.

I remember meeting him as he descended, coming off The Hook. He asked if he should wait. *"No,"* I replied confidently. *"I won't be far behind you."* And with that, we parted ways, promising to reconvene in the dining hall later. *"See you in a bit!"*

As I descended, the scree field that had seemed manageable on the way up felt treacherous on the way down. Now warmed by the sun, the rocks were loose and threatened to send me tumbling. I was petrified.

Carefully, I took a half step laterally to my right, but suddenly, the ground gave way, and I found myself in a landslide. Miraculously, I kept my feet pointed downhill as I clawed frantically at the scree. It felt like the only thing left to stop me was a pile of rocks and trees waiting at the bottom. Yet, in that moment of chaos, as I cried out a desperate prayer, I found a reserve of strength I didn't know I had. Call it faith, call it grit—it was there. And it kept me alive as I managed to halt my slide.

When the dust settled, and the rocks stopped cascading down, I found myself battered and bruised but still alive. My harrowing slide had taken me on a fifty-foot ride, ripping up my legs and arms. I was now forty feet from a graveyard of boulders and rocks that had lost their grip on the mountain long before me. Blood trickled down my face, arms, and legs from the cuts. My left leg throbbed with excruciating pain.

Despite the agony, I found a way to traverse down that rocky slope and then assess my injuries. My head ached, but it was my left leg that was in the worst shape. As I poured water on my cuts, I saw that a chunk of my left quad was shredded. It was a deep cut. I used an extra shirt to clean and cover my wounds and hobbled my way back into camp an hour later.

Entering the empty dining hall covered in dried blood and dirt, I was greeted by the lingering aroma of a meal I had missed. A person came out of the kitchen to clean tables, saw me, and immediately stopped to assist me. They cleaned me up. A few minutes later, my climbing partner appeared. He had saved me a plate. It was a small gesture that spoke volumes.

Later, Tom Hemingway, the director of the Spring Canyon Retreat and Conference Center, spent some time with me to make sure I was okay. After hearing my story, and seeing that I was alright, he offered some words of wisdom.

"You almost lost your life when you faced the mountain today," he said solemnly. *"You took a severe fall, yet you're still here. Do you realize that every day forward is now a gift? The question is, what will you do with that gift?"*

I was seventeen years old when that happened, and those words stuck with me long after the bruises had faded. While I understood their significance then, it's only now that I fully grasp their depth. They reveal a surprising truth about resilience: faith and grit are essential not just for *facing the mountain*, but for changing the world. This lesson is crucial because we all have mountains to face. And who wouldn't want to change the world?

◆　◆　◆

This book is for anyone facing a mountain—a significant challenge they want to overcome. It's also for those who want to support others through challenges. I invite you to join me on this journey. By the end of the book, I will share more about how the events on The Hook shaped my life.

None of us are meant to be the tailings at the bottom of the hill; we are each meant to be vital building blocks for impact. In the pages ahead, we will explore compelling stories of resilience and practical tips to persevere in both business and life. As you read, I encourage you to capture your thoughts in a companion journal.

While we talk about faith and grit (and I do share how my faith has supported me), it's important to understand that this isn't a religious book; it's a resilience book.

Only in the face of challenges do we discover our strength and resolve. Even when life feels like a landslide, we can find our way back to the path. That is the essence of facing the mountain. Resilience is finding our foothold despite the challenge. And it all starts with a simple question:

What mountain are YOU facing?

2 – LIFE IN THREE ACTS

In 1910, Teddy Roosevelt, the former President of the United States, traveled to Europe to deliver his acceptance speech for the Nobel Peace Prize. He had won the prize four years earlier for his role in helping to end the war between Japan and Russia.

To maximize the trip, he accepted a speaking invitation at Sorbonne University in Paris. Roosevelt titled his talk, "Citizenship in a Republic." Midway through, he delivered one of the most inspiring messages of our era, now immortalized as *The Man in the Arena*.

"It is not the critic who counts;
not the man who points out how the strong man stumbles,
or where the doer of deeds could have done them better.

The credit belongs to the man who is actually in the arena,
whose face is marred by dust and sweat and blood;
who strives valiantly;

who errs, who comes short again and again,
because there is no effort without error and shortcoming;
but who does actually strive to do the deeds;

who knows the great enthusiasms, the great devotions;
who spends himself in a worthy cause;

who at the best knows in the end the triumph of high
achievement, and who at the worst, if he fails,
at least fails while daring greatly,
so that his place shall never be with those cold and timid
souls who neither know victory nor defeat."[1]

Let's face it, we all encounter "mountains." These mountains can take various forms—an overwhelming problem or project, a difficult season of life, an unexpected event, a challenging relationship, a financial crisis, a global pandemic, and more. *The Man in the Arena* offers a powerful depiction of resilience, encouraging us when we face these mountains. It emphasizes the importance of taking action and being engaged in life.

Three key players exist in the arena:

- The gladiator in the arena who faces the elements,
- The critic who passes judgment, and
- The spectators who passively observe.

We have all likely taken on these roles at some point in our lives. However, the focus remains on the gladiator in the arena—the doer—who may encounter failure or get caught in a landslide. The gladiator is YOU.

Despite the critics and bystanders, envision yourself persevering and tackling the mountain-like challenges head-on.

When we face our mountains with the belief that we will overcome them—combined with the determination to succeed no matter how long it takes or how tough it gets—we will find the resilience to keep moving forward in the arena.

We will refer to *The Man in The Arena* throughout this book. It's an important message that conveys the mindset required to *Face the Mountain*. However, I want to suggest that there is one more participant in the arena who is not explicitly mentioned in Roosevelt's speech: the coach or mentor who guides the gladiator.

Perhaps Roosevelt himself is the unspoken guide in this story. At some point, each of us encounters someone who helps mentor and guide us through challenges. For me, even if it was only for a summer, that person was Lieutenant Colonel Tom Hemingway. He taught me and demonstrated through his actions a values-based mental model that can significantly strengthen our resilience—no matter who we are.

The 3Cs of Resilience

I first introduced you to Tom Hemingway in the previous chapter. He was the camp director overseeing operations at Spring Canyon in Colorado, where I worked as a teenager during the summer that I took that nasty slide down the mountain. Looking back now, I see him as a mentor in my life. Hemingway exemplified the values of hard work, service, and leadership. But long before he became a guide to help others—and a leader of leaders—Hemingway had to confront his own inner critic in the arena.

Hemingway graduated from the Citadel in 1960 and was commissioned as an officer in the U.S. Marine Corps. As a young Lieutenant during the Vietnam conflict, Hemingway was given command of an infantry platoon, which would be his first significant leadership role as an officer.

An infantry platoon consists of three or four squads, each comprising between twenty to fifty soldiers. Generally, there is one officer and forty enlisted men. The most senior enlisted member serves as the operations chief alongside the officer. His rank is Gunnery Sergeant, but he is often called Gunny, for short, and out of respect for the rank.

Hemingway quickly realized that the Gunny of his platoon was a certified legend who had served in multiple conflicts, both the Pacific Theater during World War II (including Guadalcanal and Iwo Jima) and the Korean War (including Inchon and Chosin Reservoir).

Imagine how the young Lieutenant felt as he looked at his platoon roster. Nearly all these enlisted men seemed to have more experience than he did. He must have felt like he was out of his league, experiencing more than a touch of Impostor Syndrome. He was aware enough to know that whatever doubts his men had about him were at least equal to his own doubts.

Fortunately, Hemingway had the fortitude to approach his Gunnery Sergeant and seek his guidance. Swallowing hard, he shared his apprehension. *"Gunny, look, you know my background, and I know yours. I have no idea how I am supposed to lead you and these veteran Marines successfully."*[2] As Hemingway finished his sentence, Gunny instructed him to sit down. He looked him straight in the eye and said in a firm voice,

"Lieutenant, there are only three questions that I'm going to be asking about YOU and that your Marines are going to be asking about YOU."[3]

Hemingway was about to receive a lesson that would transform him for the rest of his life.

Pardon the Interruption

Before we dig deeper into the story, I have to ask: Have you ever had one of those moments, like Hemingway's, that demanded your undivided attention? For me, such a moment occurred during my high school track days—specifically, every time an official with a raised starting gun shouted: *"Racers, take your mark!"*

If you were in that race—the gladiator in the arena—you knew you were about to *face the mountain*. And let me tell you, it was also the exact moment when I suddenly felt an urgent need to pee. Every. Single. Time.

I'll never forget crouching in the starting blocks, placing my fingers on the line, and staring down the lane. Ten hurdles stood between me and the finish. But it was the first hurdle that looked like Mount Everest—that was the mountain. It felt like doubt was right there breathing in the lane next to me, talking smack. To perform at my best, I needed to imagine something greater than doubt's whispers. I needed faith that I could do it! But I also needed grit, a quality my coach drilled into us.

Coach Windsor was my Gunny on the track. For him, grit meant giving everything you had, starting at the sound of the gun, and continuing well past the finish line. Grit was about going all in and getting it done. And when that gun finally sounded, fear magically left my body. But I'd be lying if I said it wasn't a battle of nerves up until that split second before the bang. Honestly, I probably burned more calories from anxiety than from the actual race!

I can't help but imagine young Lieutenant Hemingway battling the same kind of doubt and anxiety, wondering how he would lead his platoon in the days ahead. He felt green and inexperienced—maybe even inadequate. Doubt whispered in his ear, just like it did to me at the starting blocks. But Gunny was about to flip that script for him, just like Coach Windsor did for me.

Back to the Story

Remember, Hemingway was looking for some guidance. He was about to take command of a platoon, but knew he lacked experience. While he technically outranked Gunny and could have given him orders, Hemingway was instead unassuming. Hemingway owned his ignorance and, in a moment of vulnerability, went to the veteran Gunny, who didn't pull any punches in his response.

Gunny is direct. But he's not the critic; he's the coach.

> *"The first question WE are going to ask is: Do YOU know your job, or are YOU at least striving really hard to learn it?"*[4]

Hemingway listened intently, nodding his head. But I imagine the critic inside amplified the self-doubt. *"Do I know my job? Well. Maybe. But maybe not? Am I striving hard to learn it? Yes! But am I doing enough?"*

Gunny could have poured salt on the wound, but instead clarified intent.

> *"We know you don't know everything, but we're going to be watching to see if YOU are paying attention, whether YOU are asking the right questions, and whether YOU are humble enough to find out how to do your job really, really well!"*[5]

Like a sponge, Hemingway soaked it all in. The word that came to mind for him was COMPETENCE. Gunny was challenging him to strive to be competent.

Gunny continued,

> *"The second question WE are going to ask is: Are YOU going to make the hard but right decision even if it costs YOU personally?"*[6]

Again, Hemingway listened intently to Gunny. I imagine the critic inside questioned his resolve. *"Do I have the courage and wisdom? I think so. But the proof is in the pudding. Time will tell."*

The second word that came to mind for Hemingway after his reflection was now COURAGE. Gunny was challenging him to be courageous.

Courage means to face the challenge head-on and to step forward despite the fear. It's about leaping out of the blocks when the gun goes off.

Gunny then wrapped it up,

> *"The third question WE are going to ask is: Do YOU care as much about me and these guys as YOU care about yourself?"*[7]

At this point, Hemingway likely had an epiphany. He was already mulling over COMPETENCE and COURAGE, but now this question must have intrigued him the most—maybe even excited him. *"Do I care for them—more than me? I do. There's no doubt. I do. That's how I like to be led, and that's how I want to lead."*

The third word that came to mind for Hemingway was COMPASSION. Gunny was challenging him to show compassion to those whom he would lead.

This is probably the one word that would shape Hemingway more than any other, at least for the time I knew him and what others have shared about him.

Compassion is about genuinely caring for the well-being of others and feeling driven to take action to meet a need. It's recognizing that life isn't about you and how you appear; it's about the impact you have on those around you.

Needless to say, these three qualities from Gunny would serve as a catalyst for Tom Hemingway's 3Cs:

- Competence
- Courage
- Compassion

The mountains we face are a proving ground for the 3Cs; they are what shape us. If we are in the arena, striving to dare greatly, the 3Cs of Resilience will be the measures of our success. This is how we find victory—but victory only comes to those who *face the mountain*. The mountain sharpens our Competence, tests our Courage, and deepens our Compassion. Only by facing the mountain can we dare to change the world.

The Theory of Resiliency

Perhaps Albert Einstein is best known for his *Theory of Relativity,* which connects energy (E), mass (M), and the speed of light (C), expressed in the famous equation:

$$E = MC^2$$

Einstein's theory suggests that time travel is possible, which could be a phenomenal shortcut to resilience. *But how would this work?*

If objects—like you and me—could move near the speed of light, we would experience time more slowly, a phenomenon known as "time dilation." That would certainly make you and me more resilient. While time dilution would be super cool, without a DeLorean equipped with a flux capacitor, it's pretty much out of reach.

Fortunately, there's a practical equation we can use today, which I call *The Theory of Resiliency.*

$$I = 3C^T$$

Just as Einstein connected energy, mass, and light speed, the *Theory of Resiliency* illustrates how resilience—multiplied by the 3Cs and fueled by the power of time (T)—can be transformational in overcoming challenges. With steady effort the 3Cs cultivate the faith and grit needed to make an impact. But it takes time.

◆　◆　◆

Resilience is the ability to adapt, recover, and grow stronger in the face of mountains. *But how do we build it?*

By applying Competence, Courage, and Compassion powered over Time, we learn to navigate challenges, climb mountains, and create lasting impact. This formula emphasizes how patience and persistence work together.

The 3Cs:

- **Competence:** Deliver results through skill, knowledge, and experience. *Keep Learning.*

- **Courage:** Act boldly, even in the face of fear, and uncertainty. *Be Bold.*

- **Compassion:** Show empathy and care, driving a purpose beyond self-interest. *Honor Others.*

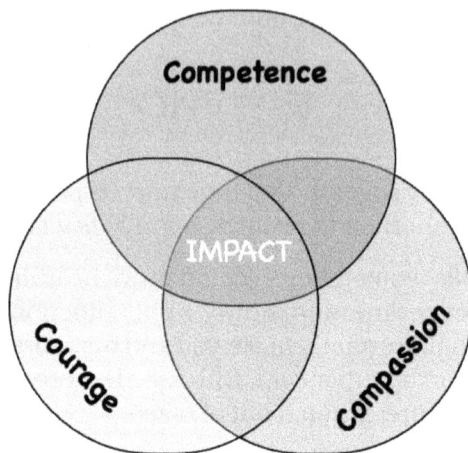

Figure 1 – The Measurables of Resilience

These qualities define those who face the mountain. The 3Cs work best in parallel, not sequentially, forming the foundation of every great resilience story. Time plays a vital role by creating experience and marking consistent effort. It amplifies the 3Cs exponentially, showing that impact is cumulative. The more consistent the commitment, the greater the impact.

If any of the 3Cs is missing—Competence, Courage, or Compassion—the impact diminishes, similar to how Einstein's theory of relativity fails if mass (M) or speed of light (C) is zero. This framework shows that leadership and growth require sustained effort, not just moments of brilliance.

As we become more resilient, our impact grows exponentially. Competence, Courage, and Compassion—when practiced together—have the power to change the world.

ACT ONE – Competence

*"Do YOU know your job, or are YOU at least
striving really hard to learn it?"*
– Gunny

ompetence is the ability to do something effectively and efficiently, drawing on the necessary skills, knowledge, and potential to perform a task to a high standard. But it's important to understand no one starts out competent. From the moment we are born, we begin the journey of learning—how to breathe, how to crawl before walking, and how to walk before running. This journey embodies the *Face the Mountain* mindset: believing we can withstand the storms ahead, even if we don't yet know how.

Competence is not innate; it's nurtured and built over time. It involves constant learning and improvement, making it a journey, not a destination. As we develop our skills, gain experience, and achieve success, we build confidence in our ability to face adversity. This growing competence strengthens our problem-solving and decision-making abilities, allowing us to rely on past successes and lessons learned to overcome new obstacles.

In the context of resilience, competence becomes our foundation. It's the accumulated experience and mastery that foster a belief in our own capacity to handle future setbacks. By building and maintaining competence, we not only boost our confidence but also reinforce our resilience.

In the chapters ahead, we will explore the ABCs of COMPETENCE to guide us on this journey.

- **Anticipate the Storms:** Preparing for challenges before they arise.

- **Build on Beliefs:** Strengthening the mindset that fuels our competence.

- **Commit to Duty:** Following through with the tasks at hand, no matter the difficulty.

Let's dive in and explore how developing our competence fortifies our resilience and prepares us for the mountain!

3 – ANTICIPATE THE STORMS

There's a warning label for life that most ignore. We often think it's meant for others, but it's intended for you and me. *"Here on earth, you will have many trials and sorrows."*[8]

This warning can be found in the Bible. They are the words of Jesus. His statement has often intrigued me—even when I was a kid. I could imagine his disciples thinking, *"Wait. What? Did he say trials and sorrows? I gave up my fishing net to sign up for this. I thought he came to save the world!"* However, Jesus spoke with honesty, seeking to prepare his disciples—and all of us—for the challenges ahead.

It echoes what the ancient Homer shares in his epic poem, *The Iliad*, one of the oldest recorded literary works.

"The roaring seas and many a dark range of mountains lie between us."[9]

While *The Iliad* contains this warning of difficult seas and mountains ahead, I find *The Odyssey*, Homer's other renowned work, even more captivating. It follows Odysseus's harrowing journey home after the war as he faces numerous obstacles. These trials and sorrows ultimately shape him for life.

One of Odysseus's companions is an older man named Mentor. This is where we are first introduced to the term *mentor*, commonly used today. Mentor's role was to impart wisdom and knowledge. The etymology of the word *mentor* defines it as a "wise advisor," an intimate friend who is a sage counselor.

Think back to the mentors of your youth. How did they prepare you for the journey? Did they equip you and ready you for the challenges that lay ahead? More importantly, were you listening?

The Storms of Life

Most mentors tried to prepare us, although we were not always anxious to listen. The books they suggested tried to alert and equip us, yet most of us hoped we could somehow dodge the storms and battles.

But guess what? We can't. They are inevitable. Each of us must learn to *face the mountain.*

Life involves pain and adversity; competence never comes easy. I could fill pages with my story, recounting unexpected challenges, setbacks, and heartbreaks, some of which put me flat on my back or almost at the bottom of a mountain. I'm sure you have yours, too. The question isn't, *"Did I fall down?"* The question to ask is, *"Did I get back up?"* That's what matters most.

Circumstances don't define us; the choices we make in the midst of them do.

J. R. R. Tolkien is widely accepted as one of the greatest storytellers ever. If you read *The Lord of the Rings* or saw one of the movies, you know that Tolkien uses fiction to expose the truth so that we can discover something greater.

Tolkien tells the tale of Frodo, a hobbit who possesses a dangerous artifact identified as the One Ring. The One Ring is a source of immense power. It grants its bearer invisibility, but also exerts a corruptive influence. It serves as a symbol of evil that needs to be destroyed. The only way to dispose of the One Ring is to journey to the distant mountain where it was forged and cast it into the mountain's fire.

Joining Frodo on his journey are his best friend, Sam; two other hobbits named Merry and Pippin, who are both very clever; the dwarf Gimli, a skilled warrior; the elf Legolas, a master archer; two descendants of royalty in Boromir and Aragorn, both well-regarded warriors; and the wizard Gandalf. Together, they form the Fellowship of the Ring, and their mission is to help Frodo travel to Mount Doom to dispose of the One Ring.

Along the way, they encounter multiple storms and battles on their quest, and not all make it. One storm takes the great Gandalf out of play. But guess what? He comes back!

He reunites with Aragorn, Gimli, and Legolas. In one memorable scene from the film *The Two Towers*, Aragorn, stunned to see him return, reacts, *"It cannot be. You fell!"*[10]

Gandalf responds and tells the story. *"I threw down my enemy and smote his ruin upon the mountainside. I felt life in me again. I have been sent back."*[11]

Translation: *"I got back up."*

One of the more interesting quotes from Gandalf is during this reunion. *"A great storm is coming, but the tide has turned."*[12]

Later, in *The Return of the King*, he adds,

> *"Courage will now be your best defense against the storm that is at hand—that and such hope as I bring."*[13]

A mentor's job is to offer hope.

We will dive deeper into Courage in Act Two and explore how Compassion brings hope in Act Three. But the phrase *"hope as I bring"* particularly resonated with me. It serves as a reminder that Competence empowers us to contribute meaningfully to others, regardless of our level of experience.

Storms can be scary, but understanding the storm can help prepare us for its coming. This becomes a turning point for competence despite the storm. This is when the tide turns from fear to faith. But faith must also be coupled with grit. The two should be inseparable.

Jesse Owens – *The Man in the Arena*

One of my favorite stories of someone who fought the storms and changed the world is Jesse Owens.

No critic was greater than the one Jesse faced in the 1936 Berlin Olympics: Adolf Hitler. Hitler and his Third Reich wanted nothing more than to see Owens, a Black man, fail. But Owens shocked the world by taking home four gold medals for Team USA. He proved that talent, determination, and the human spirit transcend racial and ideological barriers, directly challenging Hitler's vision of Aryan supremacy.[14]

Born the son of a sharecropper, Owens was a dreamer with a powerful imagination. After his family moved from Alabama to Cleveland, Ohio, he began pursuing his dream. At fourteen, he started running in junior high, quickly gaining local media attention. In high school, he set multiple state and national records and was recruited by Ohio State.

Despite not receiving a scholarship, he worked nights and weekends to support himself and his wife, Ruth. Juggling school, work, and marriage was no easy feat—especially when you're breaking world records on the side!

Owens carried three intangible assets: imagination, faith, and grit. Though he was a dreamer, it was his faith and grit that allowed him to persevere and seize every opportunity.

During his senior year at Ohio State, at the 1935 Big Ten Championships, just days after injuring his back in a fall at home, Owens wasn't sure he could compete. His coach suggested taking it one event at a time, starting with the 100-yard dash to test his back. To everyone's surprise, Owens not only won but tied the world record at 9.4 seconds. Despite the pain, he went on to set world records in all four of his events that day.

Resilience was in Owen's DNA. He faced a tough decision: boycott the Berlin Olympics because of Hitler's position on race or to pursue his calling. Owens chose to compete despite the fear.

After his Olympic successes on the track, Owens became an inspirational speaker, encouraging others to pursue their dreams. He once shared,

> *"The battles that count aren't the ones for gold medals. The struggles within yourself—the invisible, inevitable battles inside all of us—that's where it's at."*[15]

He also said,

> *"We all have dreams. But in order to make dreams come into reality, it takes an awful lot of determination, dedication, self-discipline, and effort."*[16]

In other words, competence requires faith and grit.

Understanding Faith and Grit

Each of us learns to stand before we walk. The competence to stand demands resilience from the start. With faith and grit, we not only learn to walk but also get back up if we fall. Faith is belief. Grit drives action. Action fosters growth. Growth builds experience. Experience develops competence. And competence breeds confidence.

The Oxford English Dictionary defines *faith* as a noun signifying *"complete trust or confidence in someone or something."*[17] While accurate, I find this definition uninspiring. It's missing the connection to grit. A more dynamic perspective comes from the Bible: *"Faith is the assurance of things hoped for, the conviction of things not seen."*[18]

This definition uses the terms *assurance* and *conviction*, implying that faith must be followed through. Faith isn't just a wish; it's a vision carried out. A wish is something we want but aren't committed to pursuing. In contrast, a vision is something we believe in and feel we must act on. That's why faith needs grit. Faith also involves trust—trust in the vision, in ourselves, and in the process. It requires believing in the unseen and taking steps toward it, confident that our actions will bring the vision to life.

The Bible, one of the oldest books of all time, is a reference point for reality. Ronald Reagan, America's fortieth president, once remarked, *"Inside its pages lay all the answers to all the problems man has ever known."*[19]

Reagan added, *"It's my firm belief that the enduring values . . . presented in its pages have a great meaning for each of us and for our nation. The Bible can touch our hearts, order our minds, and refresh our souls."*[20]

Many of my mentors adhered to the Bible's definition of faith, yet interestingly, not all were religious. For instance, my track coach encouraged us to envision what's possible, emphasizing the importance of setting clear goals and maintaining hope. He instilled in us the conviction to persevere with faith and grit despite doubt.

Others, like Hemingway, who was deeply biblical, taught me to recognize potential and actively seek it out. While many were different in their spoken beliefs, their mindsets were similar.

I also remember my dad guiding me during my early college days. There were several classes where I struggled. But occasional calls with Dad reminded me about the importance of grit—taking action despite not seeing the whole picture. He often told me, *"The answer to a problem doesn't always reveal itself until after you start working on it."* Those moments eliminated my excuse to procrastinate.

Grit is stamina on steroids. It is the ability to persevere through something that might be difficult. Grit is enduring without giving way; it's a core component of the *Face the Mountain* mindset. Faith starts with belief, and grit keeps our faith going when the battle gets tough. Grit reminds us that the answer requires effort to be achieved.[21]

In mountaineering, you ascend a hill with faith, believing there's an awe-inspiring view and a personal achievement at the top. However, grit is required to get you there.

Grit is the work it takes to live out our faith. It's pursuing our calling, overcoming the hurdle in front of us, and then tackling the next and then the next.

Faith and grit go hand in hand, sparking belief and driving action. With faith comes confidence that something meaningful and fulfilling lies beyond every mountain. With grit, we develop the courage to expend effort to get there, even when it seems impossible. Together, faith and grit equip us to face any challenge, even when we stumble.

The Four Seasons

Every story of success comes with a storm or two. But there is no storm that faith and grit can't get us through. As Jim Rohn shares in his book *The Four Seasons of Life*, we often experience these storms as different seasons:

Spring - a time of blessings and new beginnings.

Spring feels like blue-sky days that may never end. It's a time for planting new ideas and being excited about fresh opportunities. The storms of spring are often refreshing showers that help things grow. We feel energized. But spring can suddenly bring rain that makes us feel drenched or overwhelmed. The key is to pace ourselves, appreciate the beauty, and know when to seek cover.

Summer - a time to protect and nurture.

Summer is when we might experience heat, drought, thunderstorms, or even tornadoes. The storms of summer can be jarring, threatening the seeds we planted in spring. It's a season of hardship and discouragement, where we feel the heat, sweat, and fatigue from our efforts.

Fall - the time for harvesting the fruits of our labor.

Fall is a time of gathering and often celebrating after the trials of summer. Yet, the storms in this season can catch us off guard, striking us like a tornado or hurricane. We might feel like we've lost our harvest or that our foundation has been shaken. We might experience anxiety or a sense of loss.

Winter - when we might encounter the severest storms.

Winter brings loneliness, disappointment, and sometimes disaster. The days grow shorter, and the nights longer. When storms come, we must be well-prepared; otherwise, winter can feel cold, brittle and isolating. We may feel helpless, alone, or stranded. The hardships of winter often feel prolonged and unrelenting.[22]

When Life Knocks You Down

No season lasts forever; seasons change.

Think back—what unexpected seasons have you faced and survived? Maybe some were painful. Maybe you still feel the sting. Take a moment to reflect on the challenging times you've endured. Here are a few to consider:

- Loss of a loved one
- Health challenge
- Financial setback
- Relationship conflict
- Legal struggle
- Work challenge
- School struggle
- Social pressure
- Moral slip-up
- Missed opportunity
- Technology issue
- Travel delay
- Car accident
- Environmental disaster
- Global pandemic

Have any of these happened to you or someone you know? Maybe you're in the middle of one right now.

Think about the emotions these storms can stir up.

Feelings like:

- Grief
- Loneliness
- Anxiety
- Doubt
- Worry
- Bitterness
- Discontentment
- Overwhelm
- Frustration
- Exhaustion
- Sleeplessness
- Procrastination

When life hits hard, it takes a toll. These seasons can feel like mountains. But here's the good news—you don't have to climb alone. If you feel overwhelmed, consider finding a coach or mentor who has been through similar experiences and can help you navigate the storm. This book has ideas to guide you, but a coach or mentor can help you, too.

I know because I've done it. I've turned to a coach when life knocked me down or when I needed a fresh perspective. Take the ideas in this book and use them in conversation with a coach, mentor, or trusted friend who can help you stand tall again.

Life is challenging. We all bear the marks of dust, sweat, and tears. But with the right help, you can get through it—you can get back up!

Remember, it's never over unless you choose to quit!

Preparing for the Storm

The most influential person in world history is arguably Jesus. He brought hope and life to people and taught them the value of forgiveness. Yet, he didn't always feed people words of bliss and blessing or sugar-coat reality.

During his short time on Earth, Jesus, as a leader, often told people not what they wanted to hear but what they needed to hear. That could sometimes sting. But remember, mentors are there to guide and instruct. Beyond our own experiences, mentors are our best teachers. It's how the tide turns.

Here are four lessons to help us face adversity and build competence.

Lesson #1 – Know What's Coming

Curious about the dangers we face, I began exploring written warnings, starting with the Bible. I was surprised that a book about hope contains so many forewarnings of trouble. Here are just a few:

- *You will grow tired and weary.*[23]
- *You will sweat all your life to earn a living.*[24]
- *You will be attacked.*[25]
- *You will suffer.*[26]
- *People will oppose you.*[27]
- *You will be hard-pressed on every side.*[28]
- *You will face trials and sorrows.*[29]

That's some hard stuff to swallow. It almost sounds like source material for an Allstate commercial: *Mayhem will happen. Are you ready?*

Storms have been forewarned throughout history, but we likely won't find these warning labels posted as a social media meme. Fear might sell, but what we need is more faith and grit. That's why I wrote this book—to focus on the value of facing the mountain instead of avoiding it, especially when growth awaits on the other side. The next step is preparation.

Lesson #2 – Brace for Impact

Fortunately, there is some good news—all that gloom and doom can be defused. When mayhem happens, there's no need to cower, hide, or bury our head in the sand. There is a way to persevere.

First, we are more resilient when we anticipate the storm. Think of it like braving an ocean wave. When you step into the water and see the wave approaching, you brace yourself and step into it. If not, the wave will knock you back. By stepping forward, you are ready for impact—and you move through it.

Secondly, recognize that it's not the storm that destroys us; it's our response to it. If we react with *apathy*—neglecting to care—we leave things to chance, which can have devastating consequences. If we choose *aversion*—avoiding the storm—we might dodge the hurricane but miss the growth that comes with the struggle. Sometimes, to see the sunshine, we must *anticipate* the storm.

A common tendency is to be frozen by fear, which can severely limit us. However, if our response is one of awareness—anticipating and preparing for the storm—we stand a better chance. We can either step into the wave with intention or seek shelter until we are ready to brave the elements. Either way, preparation allows us to *face the mountain*.

Speaking of awareness, consider the storms and seasons you've endured. Can you identify a few? I can recall several near-death experiences growing up—times I shouldn't have made it. I've also faced some health challenges, yet here I am, still moving forward. *How is that possible?*

What storm has disrupted your life? Did you make it through? Maybe it's something you are fighting through right now. But remember this—you are still here! Surviving those storms indicates you are meant to be here. There's a purpose for you, no matter what the past holds.

Knowing we've endured storms before offers hope for the future. It means we are resilient!

It also means that "impossible" is just an illusion.

Lesson #3 – Imagine It Possible

One of my favorite questions is, "*What would you do if you knew you couldn't fail?*" But an even better question might be, "*What could you accomplish if you knew you were meant to try?*" Would you remain stuck, or would you discover some breakthroughs?

Despite the Bible's warning about storms, it also shares a powerful message that with faith, *"Nothing is ever impossible."*[30] When faced with what seems like impossible odds, we should remember this. For those who *face the mountain*, impossible becomes an invitation to try.

A similar message is conveyed in Tim Burton's 2010 adaptation of Lewis Carroll's classic, *Alice in Wonderland*. In this version, a nineteen-year-old Alice is transported back into a mysterious underworld, now ruled by the oppressive Red Queen.

Determined to end the tyranny, Alice embarks on a journey to the Towering Peak of Possibility, where she must slay a ferocious monster named Jabberwocky to save Wonderland.

At first Alice is timid, thinking it's impossible. But she summons up the courage, recalling the inspiring words of her father, Charles Kingsleigh:

> *"The only way to achieve the impossible*
> *is to believe it is possible."*[31]

With renewed hope, Alice faces the Jabberwocky, recounting the seemingly impossible things she has witnessed until she finally slays this monster and frees Wonderland.

This idea that "impossible" is within our reach was also the central message of an Adidas ad campaign from the early 2000s, featuring these words of Muhammed Ali.

> *"Impossible is just a big word thrown around by small*
> *men who find it easier to live in the world they've been*
> *given than to explore the power they have to change it.*
> *Impossible is not a fact. It's an opinion.*
> *Impossible is not a declaration. It's a dare.*
> *Impossible is potential.*
> *Impossible is temporary.*
> *Impossible is nothing."*[32]

Lesson #4 – Step Out of The Comfort Zone

The mountains we face—and the storms that come with them—are what help push us out of our comfort zone and into our potential zone, our Towering Peak of Possibility.[33]

It's only when we step out of our comfort zone that we can truly position ourselves to achieve the impossible.

Here's something else to consider: if you think it's impossible, you are probably right. But if you think there's even a slight chance it's possible, then why not?

Think about Jesse Owens. He needed faith and grit to be resilient. Or the Wright brothers and their sister Katharine, who believed in something others thought was impossible. Consider Gertrude Ederle, the first woman to swim across the English Channel despite being told it couldn't be done.

Remember Roger Bannister breaking the 4-minute mile. Or the Founding Fathers of the United States, defying impossible odds to establish a new nation. And think about David defeating Goliath.

Facing the mountain often means being willing to do what others say is impossible. But does that mean YOU should think it's impossible?

You won't know how far you can go unless you *face the mountain*.

What could you accomplish if you were meant to try?

◆　◆　◆

Before we end this chapter, I'd like to share a poem my wife discovered while working on her book, *Permission to Be Bold*. The poem is titled *Good Timber* by Douglas Malloch, and it beautifully illustrates how storms can strengthen trees, symbolizing our own growth and resilience.

Like the trees in the poem, we too are fortified by challenges when we step out of our comfort zones. The storms we face are not obstacles; they fortify us.

I hope you find it as powerful and inspiring as I do.

GOOD TIMBER

by Douglas Malloch

The tree that never had to fight
For sun and sky and air and light,
But stood out in the open plain
And always got its share of rain,
Never became a forest king
But lived and died a scrubby thing.

The man who never had to toil
To gain and farm his patch of soil,
Who never had to win his share
Of sun and sky and light and air,
Never became a manly man
But lived and died as he began.

Good timber does not grow with ease:
The stronger wind, the stronger trees;
The further sky, the greater length;
The more the storm, the more the strength.
By sun and cold, by rain and snow,
In trees and men, good timbers grow.

Where thickest lies the forest growth,
We find the patriarchs of both.
And they hold counsel with the stars
Whose broken branches show the scars
Of many winds and much of strife.
This is the common law of life.[34]

Action Steps

What if I told you that we're not only meant to survive the storms but to thrive because of them? The storms we encounter serve two purposes:

- They reveal our character (who we are).

- They fortify our strength (who we will become).

This chapter focuses on preparing for the storms and seasons we face. We are meant to be resilient. Like *The Man in the Arena,* we are meant to get back up and continue fighting. That's the essence of resilience.

Competence is achieved by stepping out of our comfort zone and *facing the mountain.* It doesn't come naturally; it's forged in life's trials, much like steel. Remember, whatever season you're in, it won't last forever. Seasons change.

Here are some action steps to help you navigate seasonal changes and storms:

1. *Expect the Unexpected*

Be prepared for surprises and uncertainties, and events you can't foresee. Embrace the belief that you can overcome any storm, mountain, or season. Use your past experience as proof of your resilience. Reflect on moments when you triumphed despite doubts—yours and others.

2. *Acknowledge How Adversity Has Strengthened You*

Look back at the mountains you've climbed. Do you see yourself as a victim or a victor? Your story can inspire others. With humility, share your victories; they may not mean much to you, but they could mean everything for someone else.

No one becomes competent without enduring challenges. Just as a strong tree grows resilient from the wind, the mountains you face will make you stronger. This is essential for developing true competence.

4 – BUILD ON BELIEF

"Be sure you put your feet in the right place,
then stand firm."
– Abraham Lincoln

It's not the storm that's the threat; it's our response to it. We can minimize the adverse effects of the storm in two ways: believing we will get through it, which is *faith*, and doing what we must, which is *grit*.

These two elements strengthen our COMPETENCE, and the next step in facing the mountain centers on this core element of *belief.*

Jackie Robinson – *The Birth of a Legend*

Belief reflects what we value. When our values align, our vision becomes clear. This concept is powerfully illustrated in the movie *42,* based on the real-life story of Jackie Robinson.

In 1946, Branch Rickey, the manager of the Brooklyn Dodgers, had a vision that challenged the norms of the time: integrating a Negro player into Major League Baseball. Rickey's decision wasn't just about talent; it was a shift in values, breaking an unwritten code against integration.[35]

After evaluating candidates, Rickey chose Jackie Robinson, a multi-sport star from UCLA and a war veteran playing in the Negro Leagues. When they met in Rickey's office, Rickey posed a critical set of questions, asking Robinson if he had the resilience to endure the inevitable hostility. When Robinson's temper flared in response, questioning if Rickey wanted a player without the courage to fight back, Rickey clarified, *"No. I want a player to have the guts NOT to fight back."*[36]

Rickey warned that people would try to provoke Robinson, saying, *"Your enemy will be out in force."*[37] He emphasized that self-control and excellence on the field were the key. Moved by Rickey's conviction and call for extraordinary resilience, Robinson replied, *"Give me a uniform.*

Give me a number on my back. And I will give you the guts!"[38]

This moment marked the start of a profound transformation in baseball and American society. Despite resistance, Robinson's resilience revealed his character.

As Teddy Roosevelt stated in the full version of *The Man in the Arena* speech:

"Above mind and above body stands character."[39]

Robinson was literally the man in the arena, with critics pointing out each time he stumbled and how he could have done things better. But this legendary figure wearing the number 42 valiantly strived, committed to a worthy cause, and dared greatly.

When the door was opened a crack by someone who believed in him, he stepped through it. Because of that, he altered the course of history forever, demonstrating to the world that character starts with belief.

What Do You Value?

Beliefs represent the values that help us weather the storms. To *face the mountain* and build resilience, we must know what we believe and why. The best way to gauge our belief is by examining our behavior.

Also, pay attention to the perceptions and thoughts of others. Often, our behavior can be influenced by how we perceive others.

It's also important to consider the impact of our words and behavior. While words represent our values, our actions reflect reality; they communicate our values.

When there's a disconnect between our values and behavior, it reveals a misalignment. It's hard to stay competent when this happens. To get back on track, identify and prioritize values that matter, then commit to living them.

Here is a list of "42" target values to guide you—though there may be others to consider.[40]

Table 1 – The *FACE THE MOUNTAIN* Target Values

Accountable	Energetic	Motivating	Self-Disciplined
Adaptable	Focused	Multiplying	Strategic
Alert	Generous	Observant	Serving
Authentic	Growth-minded	Passionate	Teachable
Calm	Hopeful	Patient	Tenacious
Coachable	Humble	Prudent	Trustworthy
Communicative	Innovative	Qualified	Unifying
Courageous	Integrous	Resilient	Visionary
Diligent	Intentional	Resourceful	Vulnerable
Disciplined	Kind	Responsive	
Empathetic	Loving	Secure	

While some of these 42 words are verbs or nouns; they also function as adjectives. Adjectives shape perceptions by describing or modifying nouns. In this case, these words describe YOU and how you will *face the mountain.*

Your Top Five Values?

I suggest picking five values to define. Don't merely view them as aspirations; instead, start incorporating them into your present life as if they already define who you are.

If it's helpful, consider placing the phrase *I am* before each value. Here's an example of five values I picked using this technique:

1. *I am Tenacious.*
2. *I am Adaptable.*
3. *I am Growth-minded.*
4. *I am Innovative.*
5. *I am Trustworthy.*

To make them easy for me to remember, I've arranged these five values into an acronym—TAGIT. Feel free to creatively organize your values in a way that works for you. If selecting five values feels challenging, start with just one.

Keystone Word or Phrase

To cement these values further, take a moment to choose a keystone word or phrase to be your primary focus for the next ninety days to a year. For instance, at the end of each year, I select a new word or phrase to guide me in the upcoming year instead of making a traditional New Year's resolution. This word or phrase reflects the person I want to be and how I want to show up.

I regularly review this word or phrase, assessing how well I embody it in my actions. For instance, my chosen phrase for the present year at the time of writing is *Own It*. I use this phrase to encompass my five values as attributes I know I need to own. At the end of each day, I ask myself, *"Did I Own It? Yes, or no?"*

Do You Own It?

When I coached varsity soccer a few years back, I looked for players who were team-centered and willing to learn, revealing what they truly valued.

A player's ability matters, but availability matters more. Skills can be built, but a player's heart is much harder to train. I wanted players who were willing to learn, ready to face the storms, and committed to being there for their teammates. Values reveal what people believe and how they will show up when the storms come.

A great coach or leader lives their values in such a way that those around them can clearly see what they stand for, even if they are not perfect.

Reality #1 – Leaders Set the Example

Once, during a game, the referee missed a call that changed the outcome. Calm was not my default, and I lost my cool.

My reaction led to a yellow card. It was one of the few times I received a card as a coach. What struck me was my players' reaction. They started complaining too, causing us to lose composure. I regretted my behavior; it set the wrong example.

To this day, I wish I had handled that situation better for my players.

Reality #2 – Leaders Press On

The next day, I apologized to the team and owned my mistake. This reset our focus, and we pressed on to play some of our best games. Values are meant to be shared and understood, but it's even more crucial to demonstrate them through our actions rather than just talk about them. When we are off track, we must own it, admit the mistake, reset and move forward. That's how we truly own it.

The reset is about returning to our values. Values matter. Without clear values, we may lose our vision.

Do You Believe?

Have you ever watched *Ted Lasso* on Apple TV+, starring Jason Sudeikis? Imagine an American football coach taking over a British soccer team. It sounds pretty comical.[41] As nutty as that show is, there are some lessons to learn from Coach Lasso.

Despite knowing little of soccer, Lasso accepts the job in London, facing criticism from the press and fans, yet guides a struggling team out of mediocrity.

Early on, Lasso posts a handwritten sign on the wall: BELIEVE in all caps. It's meant to inspire the team, but also himself. The sign becomes a symbol of faith for the players, motivating them greatly. However, their spirits are crushed when they find the sign torn in half at halftime during a game. Instead of repairing it, Lasso tears it up further, shocking the team.

"It's just a sign," he tells them.

He explains they shouldn't rely on external symbols but believe in themselves and their abilities. *"BELIEVE is something that is coming from within, not from the outside."*[42]

This lesson is crucial when facing the mountain: BELIEVE in what you have inside you. It's there for a reason.

This echoes an Eleanor Roosevelt quote:

> *"The future belongs to those who believe in the beauty of their dreams."*[43]

The Science of Belief

Our thoughts and convictions significantly influence our physical and mental well-being. Research shows that beliefs directly impact cognitive processes and brain responses, shaping how we experience the world. Faith and grit enhance our resilience, reduce stress, and improve overall health.

Neuroscience, psychology, and cognitive science studies highlight that strong beliefs can shape our cognitive processes and subjective experiences, reinforcing the power of belief in shaping reality.[44]

In this case, beliefs drive behavior, pushing us to pursue our dreams and giving us purpose and possibilities despite obstacles. On the other hand, disbelief—rooted in doubt and fear—holds us back, limiting our potential. Disbelief is simply the belief that we can't or shouldn't.[45]

Inspired by Ted Lasso, we should replace limiting beliefs with empowering ones. When belief drives behavior, behavior becomes the true measure of our values. Most people won't embrace our vision until they embrace our values. That's because behavior has the power to attract or repel.

What do you believe in? And how does your behavior offer evidence of those values? What attracts and what repels?

Your EQ Toolkit

Our greatest obstacle is often our emotional attitude. That was the test that Branch Rickey gave Jackie Robinson before handing him the uniform. Attitude can jeopardize beliefs. In heated moments, our reactions can compromise our values, but they also reveal what we truly value.

The key is maintaining a steady high EQ—or *emotional quotient.* Remember, the goal here is competence; nothing impacts it more than our EQ. Our EQ floor—how low we can go—becomes apparent on tough days when our values are threatened, often leading to behavior that misaligns with our beliefs. While external factors play a role, inner beliefs shape our response. It's crucial to equip ourselves with tools ahead of time to maintain our EQ.

My friend Fu Che, a Corporate Executive Coach, says, *"The key is to acknowledge when our EQ drops and promptly take action to elevate it again. Developing the skill of being aware of and bridging the EQ Gap is crucial."*[46] With the right tools, we can reset our EQ when needed.

Here are four tools I try to carry in my EQ toolkit:

- EQ Tool #1 – Be Realistic

- EQ Tool #2 – Notice What's Right

- EQ Tool #3 – Practice the Rest Step

- EQ Tool #4 – See the Path

These tools described in the pages ahead, can help reduce frustration and increase competence.

EQ Tool #1 – Be Realistic

One of my favorite lines from *The Man in the Arena* speech is when Teddy Roosevelt makes this uncommon statement that disrupts our thinking.

"There is no effort without error and shortcoming."[47]

It's a hard truth: no matter how competent you are, you will never be perfect. This isn't about "faking it until you make it"; it's about "doing it until you make it."

Every worthwhile effort comes with challenges. If we're not facing obstacles, we're likely heading in the wrong direction. No matter how much we plan for smooth sailing, Murphy's Law will inevitably show up. Roosevelt's words remind us: to get where we need to go, we might fail a few times. But if we keep trying and getting back up, we'll get there.

"There is no effort without error and shortcoming." I found myself repeating this phrase recently during a project filled with challenges. In my initial frustration, I wanted to quit, but Roosevelt's words echoed in my mind, giving me the encouragement I needed. Instead of sinking into frustration, I latched onto faith, which fueled my grit.

Faith and grit help us override discomfort; that's how we climb the mountain.

EQ Tool #2 – Notice What's Right

In today's world, distractions and negativity can easily overwhelm us. However, by shifting our focus towards what's right rather than what's wrong, we get back on track.

This tool is more than just positive thinking—it's a powerful emotional intelligence strategy that keeps us grounded, even during challenging times. By focusing on what's right, we can navigate chaos and frustration more easily. This principle is timeless and even highlighted in the Bible.

> *"Whatever is true, whatever is honorable, whatever is just, whatever is pure, whatever is lovely, whatever is commendable, if there is any excellence, if there is anything worthy of praise, think about these things."*[48]

This passage serves as a guide, helping us stay aligned with our values and moves us closer to our vision, even in the midst of life's storms.

Negativity is loud and persistent, but what if, instead, we look for what's right? This mindset shift makes this tool a game-changer. One way to anchor this mindset is by creating prompts that remind us to see what's right.

One of my favorites is a sign I notice every day that says, *"There's always something to be thankful for."* I see this sign whenever I walk up to the office above my garage. It's a small but powerful reminder that puts me in the right frame of mind before I step into the room.

EQ Tool #3 – Practice the Rest Step

A year before my fall descending from The Hook, I was with a group climbing the south peak on Mount Princeton. That climb had a more successful outcome. I can still remember our guide's initial instructions to kick things off:

> *"Where we are walking, it's going to be steep. You are going to lose your breath. But to catch your breath, use the rest step. For every step you make, take a micro pause, breathe in, then take the next step."*

He demonstrated the rest-step mountaineering technique: a quick movement forward, followed by locking the back leg straight for a brief rest. This pattern, especially effective on inclines, repeats with every step.

Initially, I thought the rest step was a joke, meant for those out of shape. My reluctance to use it cost me halfway up the mountain, where I found myself exhausted while others, seemingly less fit, were breathing easier. Seeing my struggle, another hiker passed by and advised, *"Try the rest step."* That was all I needed. I began using it, and surprisingly, it worked! It eased my fatigue, heightened my awareness, and kept me focused.

Symbolically, the rest step offers a mental model for approaching life. What if every emotional response was matched with a micro-pause, allowing us to breathe in the goodness around us? This practice is an extension of Tool #2.

EQ Tool #4 – See the Path

This tool is about using imagination with a perspective of *hope.* Start by asking yourself: *"What is something good that I see on the other side of the* challenge?*"* Your answer reveals your faith and likely the path forward.

I believe imagination is the birthplace of innovation. It is where great ideas come to light. Innovation is about bringing to life something that adds value and impacts others. These innovations come in three forms: better products, better processes, or better people. Sometimes the best innovation is innovating ourselves. When we see the path, we see a better version of ourselves. Imagination helps us see beyond challenges.[49]

To use this tool, imagine a successful outcome. *Do you see a path, maybe even multiple paths?* Be cautious, because this is where doubt comes knocking, whispering, *"Are you sure?"*

This is when we must "Avoid the Suck." Commonly used in the military and other high-stress environments, this phrase serves as a reminder to stay alert and avoid getting trapped in demoralizing or dangerous situations. "The Suck" refers to the negative aspects of a situation—chaos, confusion, or tough circumstances—that can pull us down mentally or physically. To "Avoid the Suck" means keeping composure, and aligning decisions with values.

Acknowledge doubts but challenge them with hope. Shift your focus to ideas that help overcome Automatic Negative Thoughts

(ANTs)—the self-defeating stories we tell ourselves about what we lack. ANTs often surface when we feel "The Suck," but with hope, we can push through.[50]

Dr. Daniel Amen, a renowned psychiatrist, recommends identifying these ANTs and asking yourself if they are 100 percent true. Next, consider how you feel when experiencing the ANTs, and imagine how you would feel without them. This turnaround technique helps clarify your path and build new habits.[51] It's never too early to start thinking about how you'll reach your vision, and it's never too late to take the next step.

The Five Levels of Belief

Resilience is driven by our level of need. It's like a dial: as we face challenges, our capacity for faith and grit can actually increase. To understand this, consider Abraham Maslow's research on the five essential human needs:

1. Basic Physical Requirements
2. Safety
3. Love and Belonging
4. Recognition
5. Self-Fulfillment[52]

According to Maslow, we can only focus on higher needs once the lower ones are met. As our needs grow, so does our capacity for faith and grit. Simply put, **our resilience expands in direct proportion to the demands we face.** While there's always a floor for faith and grit, our needs set the ceiling. By understanding that our faith and grit lay the foundation, it's our needs and ambitions that push us to raise the ceiling, driving us to reach new heights and achieve what once seemed impossible.

The pursuit of life is unsustainable without resilience. Our needs drive our resolve to overcome obstacles. By applying Maslow's Hierarchy, I've discovered we can align our faith and grit with these five levels, as shown in Figure 2. Think of it as a journey map for resilience.[53]

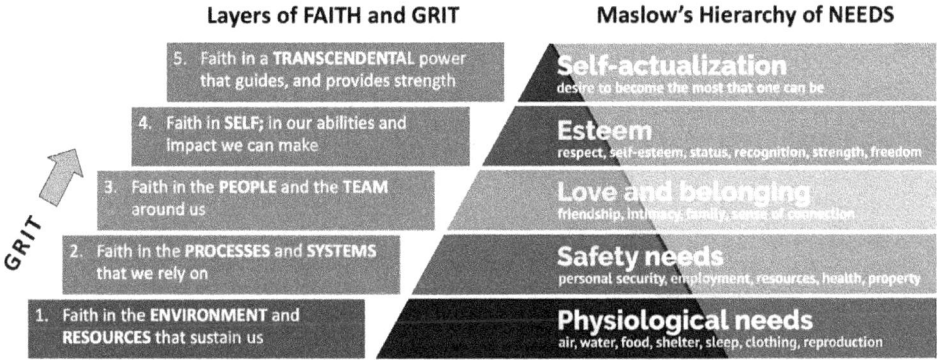

Layers of FAITH and GRIT	Maslow's Hierarchy of NEEDS

Figure 2 – The Five Levels of Belief[54]

As challenges increase, they will either blur our vision or sharpen it. The outcome depends on our belief—rooted in faith and grit. Seeking challenges that push us is crucial; to reap the rewards, we must take the risks. Ultimately, our resilience is measured by the 3Cs: Competence, Courage, and Compassion.

- **Competence** shows our readiness to handle obstacles.

- **Courage** reflects our willingness to face fears.

- **Compassion** measures our ability to connect with ourselves and others during adversity.

Together, these three qualities will reveal the depth of our belief and indicate how far our resilience can take us.

Your ability to face life's mountains is directly tied to the intensity of your belief. Let these Five Levels of Belief guide you. It's like climbing a mountain; each level demands more resilience. Human needs and struggles are universal, and belief empowers us to confront them, driving us toward our calling.

Next, let's explore these Five Levels of Belief, starting with the foundational layer and progressing to the most transcendent. Each level builds upon the last, increasing our potential impact.

Level 1 – Environment and Resources Belief

Level 1 is the foundation, where survival relies on trusting the physical infrastructure around us—like the room, chair, pathway, and essentials like food, water, and air. These elements form the bedrock of our physical well-being.

Resilient leaders operating with Level 1 faith and grit grasp the importance of these basics. They actively seek out and secure these resources, especially in environmental challenges. Whether facing a natural disaster, a resource-scarce setting, or a high-stakes mission, they prioritize the team's physical needs to establish a base for tackling complex tasks.

Leaders at this level of faith and grit recognize these necessities and ensure they are met, enabling the team to focus on the other levels.

Level 2 – Processes and Systems Belief

Level 2 is about trusting procedures and methods that yield consistent and reliable results. Processes enhance effectiveness, while systems boost efficiency. Trust in these ensures safety in both life and business.

Resilient leaders with Level 2 faith and grit understand that while established processes are crucial, adaptability is vital. They recognize that disruptions are inevitable and are quick to find new methods when necessary. By balancing trust in proven systems with the flexibility to adapt, they ensure their teams remain safe, productive, and ready to navigate change.

Transitioning from meeting basic needs to optimizing processes sets the stage for the next belief level: trust in people.

Level 3 – People and Team Belief

Level 3 is about mutual trust—trusting others and being trusted. This trust meets the need for belonging, laying the ground work for strong relationships and teamwork. At this level, building reliable and faithful relationships are essential to collaboration and success.

Resilient leaders with Level 3 faith and grit foster team trust by promoting open communication, reliability, and a shared purpose. They know that great achievements aren't made alone. They listen actively, value input, and create a safe environment for contribution, risk-taking, and innovation.

In tough times, Level 3 leaders, rally their teams by example, showing commitment and inspiring others. With clear communication, transparent decisions, and recognition, they build teams that not only survive challenges—they thrive in them.

Level 4 – Self Belief

Level 4 leaders recognize their worth and believe in their capabilities. This satisfies their itch for self-esteem and enables them to face challenges with confidence. Resilient leaders with Level 4 faith and grit draw on inner strength, and use the tools to overcome adversity. Their confidence stems from an understanding of their strengths and past experiences. They aren't easily shaken by setbacks because they trust in their ability to recover and adapt. This resilience is about thriving; not just surviving.

These leaders inspire not by being infallible but by balancing confidence with humility. They refine their skills—they prepare—knowing that competence fuels confidence, which drives their conviction to lead. In personal life or professional life, their actions reflect a belief in their purpose and abilities, uplifting those around them.

Level 5 – Transcendental Belief

Level 5 is about transcending to something greater. It involves believing in a higher power—namely, God—who guides us toward self-actualization and a sense of purpose beyond ourselves. This belief becomes the ultimate driver, providing strength and direction even in the most difficult times.

Leaders with Level 5 faith and grit maintain their influence and impact, regardless of disruptions. They embody a peace and purpose that extends beyond human effort. They operate with a deep confidence, trusting in a force greater than themselves. They don't lead alone; they lead with conviction of the heart.

Their decisions, especially in adversity, are grounded in biblically based principles. This alignment with a higher moral framework not only guides their actions but also inspires those they lead. Through prayer, reflection, or seeking wisdom from sacred texts, they draw from their faith, navigating leadership and aligning their actions with a higher purpose.

Loss of Vision

In my book *IMAGINE*, I shared about the time I lost my vision in my left eye only to find out that it was a symptom of multiple sclerosis (MS). That was a scary time. It's been said that without vision, people perish.[55]

Vision is vital for the longevity of any culture, country, or company. But we can't cast vision unless we first understand our values. This principle applies not just to individuals but also to organizations and teams. If you want a company built to last, teach the 3Cs of Resilience.

Consider once-successful companies with vision that later lost their resilience and willingness to stay in the fight. Here's a partial list:

- *Blackberry*
- *Blockbuster*
- *Borders*
- *Kodak*
- *Radio Shack*
- *Sears*

So, let's explore what happened. How did they fail?

They were successful for a long stretch but lost their vision because they became disconnected from their values.

What would have happened if each of these failed businesses had stayed focused on serving the needs of their customers and their colleagues with Competence, Courage, and Compassion? As the world changed, they didn't. Because of that, each of them suffered a landslide.

An organization can learn to thrive when it strives to satisfy the needs of those it serves. You and I are the same way. We must be relevant to stay in the fight. Values give us staying power.

A recalibration of vision with values is often necessary. People buy into the vision when they align with the values. Success is a result of those values shared, expressed, and unified. *Why?* Because values that address real needs create a common bond. If our beliefs start getting muddled, then our adopted vision might start feeling stale and not worth fighting for. Our values work to satisfy our needs; that's why it's essential to build on belief.

Putting It All Together

The Five Levels of Belief offer insight into the challenges we face and the power we hold. Consider the impact of the COVID-19 pandemic. In early 2020, we shifted focus to basic needs (Levels 1 and 2), relying on faith and grit as we stocked up on toilet paper, face masks, and hand sanitizer.

As pandemic anxiety eased, our need for connection (Level 3) resurfaced. However, have we've gotten too cozy with virtual interactions in pajama pants and Door Dash deliveries missing deeper connections in the workplace and our communities?

In a post-COVID world, our resilience may still be at risk. To rebuild, we need to push beyond our comfort zone and into the "potential zone." This means refocusing on people (Level 3) and self-improvement (Level 4).

Education is one path to self-improvement. Nelson Mandela once said, *"Education is the most powerful weapon which you can use to change the world."*[56] As seen with Mandela, education extends beyond knowledge—it deepens faith, builds grit and fosters resilience.

This choice leads to greater awareness (Level 5), extending our abilities beyond ourselves. Those at this level sense a higher power guiding them. Reaching Level 5 requires a growth mindset—consider faith that acknowledges God and grit that surpasses personal achievements.

Each Level of Belief builds upon the previous one. As we ascend the hierarchy of needs, our faith and grit strengthen. However, complacency—even for a moment—can cause us to slide back down the mountain.

Faith inspires; grit drives. But complacency threatens everything.

◆ ◆ ◆

Action Steps

Navigating seasonal changes and storms involves anchoring in our beliefs and building on that foundation. Competence is built through fuel and fire—effort and belief.

This chapter has explored the essence of resilience and the mindset needed to *Face the Mountain*. For each of the 3Cs of Resilience, different levels of faith and grit apply to life's challenges:

- **Level 1: Enhance Your Environment**. Use resources to improve your immediate surroundings. This foundational level creates a supportive environment that fosters growth.

- **Level 2: Establish Systems and Processes.** Develop systems and processes that guide your journey. These structures provide a roadmap and help maintain focus and consistency.

- **Level 3: Build a Support Network.** Connect with others for support and shared experiences. Community strengthens resolve and provides a sense of belonging.

- **Level 4: Cultivate Self-Belief.** Strengthen your confidence to push further. Belief in your abilities is crucial for overcoming obstacles and achieving success.

- **Level 5: Aim for Greater Impact.** Think beyond yourself to make a meaningful impact. Align your skills and actions with a higher purpose to fulfill a greater calling.

To navigate these levels and avoid setbacks, use the EQ Toolkit as your action steps:

1. **Be Realistic:** Set achievable goals.
2. **Notice What's Right:** Focus on positive aspects.
3. **Practice the Rest Step:** Take deliberate pauses.
4. **See the Path:** Visualize success.

Beliefs shape competence, but complacency is its enemy. Reflect on what you hold true, align your actions with those beliefs and *face the mountain* with faith and grit.

This is how you change the world!

5 — COMMIT TO DUTY

When it comes to Competence, belief alone isn't enough. Competence requires a fundamental element: commitment. Commitment instills a sense of duty, which accelerates the growth of competence.

A pivotal moment of commitment occurs when we discover our calling—a vision of our intended path. For example, Tom Hemingway found his calling in a one-on-one with Gunny when he received the 3Cs of Resilience. Jesse Owens's college coach, Larry Snyder, instilled in him the belief that he could win in the Olympics by relentlessly pushing himself to improve his technique and fostering unwavering confidence in his abilities. Jackie Robinson found his calling when Branch Rickey offered him a major league contract despite the naysayers.

Another example is reflected in the life of Joseph Jacobson, who, despite being sold into slavery as a teenager and then exiled to a foreign land, grew into one of the most influential leaders of all time.

Joseph Jacobson – *Unlikely World Leader*

Joseph's story began in a dysfunctional family. His father, a con artist, deceived his own father, stole from his brother, and fled to a foreign land. There, he manipulated a relative into giving him livestock and marrying both his daughters.

His dad would end up having thirteen children with four different women. Tragically, Joseph's mom died giving birth to his younger brother, Ben, leaving their aunt to raise the thirteen children.

Joe, as his brothers would call him, was clearly his father's favorite, a symbol of the wife he had lost. This favoritism stoked jealousy among the half-brothers, leading to dysfunction. Their resentment boiled over when Joe, who was a dreamer, told them that one day they would bow down to him. Furious, they plotted to kill him, but instead sold him into slavery. His father believed Joe was dead, and was devastated, thinking he had been killed by a wild animal.

But Joe was miles away, in a foreign land, earning respect as a slave for a high-ranking official. However, trouble followed when the official's wife, attracted to Joe, tried to seduce him. After rejecting her advances, she falsely accused him of inappropriate actions, leading to his imprisonment. Despite this injustice, Joe remained resilient, growing in competence and gained a reputation for interpreting dreams. Somehow, this caught the attention of the king.

Summoned by the king, Joe interpreted two troubling dreams, foretelling a devastating famine. His wisdom and competence impressed the king, who pardoned Joe, and appointed him second-in-command, tasked to save the nation.

Years into the famine, Joe's brothers arrived seeking food and supplies, unaware that the man before them, was the brother they once betrayed. As they bowed to him, Joe knew who they were and felt a mix of emotions—hurt, anger, and compassion. After testing their loyalty, he revealed himself with his real name. The shock and guilt on their faces were met with Joe's forgiveness, exemplifying not just his competence, but also his courage, and compassion—the 3Cs.

Reuniting with his family, including his long-lost father, was a moment of profound healing. Jacob's years of grief turned into overwhelming joy, the son he thought was lost was now found. Through forgiveness, faith, and grit, Joseph saved his family and many others from famine, impacting the course of history.

I love this story because it exemplifies the power of faith and grit in overcoming trials. Joseph never played the victim card—he was resilient. This story, with all its soap-opera-like drama, can actually be found in the Bible and recounts Joseph's rise as a leader in Egypt during one of history's greatest famines.[57] I've given him the surname Jacobson, son of Jacob, to make this story relevant today. It's a reminder that faith and grit are essential to building the 3Cs of Resilience. And it doesn't matter whose son you are, we can all make a difference.

Joseph's reunion with his family, including his father Jacob, had a profound impact on world history. Not only did it heal deep family wounds, but it also laid the foundation for the Israelites. By saving his family, Joseph established a lineage through his father Jacob and his brother Judah that eventually leads us to King David and, later, to Mary and Jesus. Imagine how different history might have been if Joseph had not been resilient.[58]

The Difference between Faith and Religion

I hesitate to bring up Bible stories because of the stereotypes they can evoke. It's easy to conflate *faith* and *religion*—they are similar but not the same. Religion, while based on faith, is a structured system of beliefs and practices shared by a community. Faith, however, is a personal trust and confidence in something greater than oneself. Both faith and religion have value, but it's often *faith* that shapes our resilience.

The Bible contains numerous stories of people like you and me who overcame incredible odds—Joseph, Esther, Daniel, Joshua, David, Ruth, and Paul, to name a few. Their resilience stemmed from their faith, not necessarily their religious activity. Their stories encourage and challenge us.

The scriptures say, *"Examine yourselves, to see whether you are in the faith."*[59] This examination brings us back to trust. It's not about knowledge, status, role, or perfect church attendance; it's about belief that drives behavior. It's about resilience, not religion.[60]

Faith is a common denominator. Everyone has faith in something, from the chair they sit in, to the team they work with, or their spiritual beliefs. Faith is about trust, confidence, and belief in something that we hope for but have not yet received. Grit, faith's companion, fuels the pursuit of that hope.

As illustrated in Figure 3, religion can be influenced by a diverse set of instructions, rules, and expectations. If we're not careful, this can lead to complacency and status quo living, confining us within the boundaries set by others. Faith, however, is powered by *imagination* and opens the door to new horizons.

Religion   Faith

Instruction   Imagination

Rules   Seeking our View of God   Seeking God's View for Us   Trust
Doctrine   Hope
Limits   Courage
Order   Exploration

Figure 3 – Religion vs. Faith

What I have come to realize is that religion often reflects man's view of God and how we should live, while faith seeks God's perspective for us. Religion is a set of organized beliefs, teachings, and practices shared by a community, whereas faith is a personal reliance on something beyond our knowledge and community.[61]

Do you see the difference?

The point is simple: faith and religion are not the same.[62] Both have their merits, but with over 4,000 variations of religion today, shaped by different cultural traditions, personal convictions, and social needs— not everyone sees God the same way.

Faith transcends the limits and barriers of common religion. It drives us to attempt what seems impossible, and with grit, we often discover it's possible after all.[63] Coincidentally, this type of faith doesn't necessarily require a belief in God. Sometimes, that belief might come later, after faith is put into action. That's because resilience starts within—it's an inside-out commitment centered on Level 4 Belief, which we need before we can ever reach Level 5. Most times belief drives behavior, but the converse can also be true. Sometimes new behavior can lead to new beliefs.

For those with the *Face the Mountain* mindset, faith and grit are about enduring, trusting, and believing in something unseen. It's about a commitment to duty—this is how competence develops.

Consider these competency-focused questions when facing the mountain:

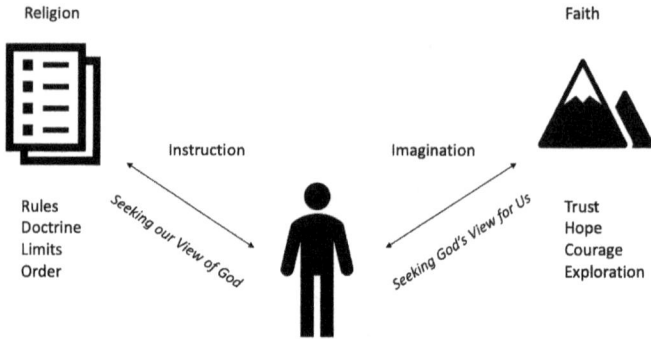

(1) What specific challenges do I face?

(2) In what do I place my trust to help me endure?

(3) What outcome do I hope for?

Reflecting on these questions reveals our *competence potential*, which is tied to both faith and grit. Faith fuels confidence, but it's grit that builds proficiency.

Answering the Call of Duty

In his preamble to his *"Man in the Arena"* speech, Teddy Roosevelt makes an intriguing declaration:

> *"Success or failure will be conditioned upon the way in which the average man and average woman, does his or her duty."*[64]

The word *duty* is significant. It signifies fulfilling obligations, commitments, and missions—an action driven by a sense of compulsion or calling.

While religion often aims to inspire obedience and obligation of duty through rules and regulations, the focus can shift when our desire to know God through faith fades and we become more focused only on strict adherence to the law. Without faith as a central anchor, religion can become more about human interpretation than divine intention.

Duty isn't just about *what* needs to be done; it's about *why* it needs to be done. The *"why"* reflects a personal conviction. This deeper sense of duty is reflected in a wide range of individuals like Jackie Robinson, Walt Disney, Michael Jordan, Mother Teresa, Martin Luther King, Jr., and Nelson Mandela, to name a few.

I hold a deep appreciation for lists. Over time, I've compiled an extensive catalog of resilient individuals who began as ordinary but accomplished the extraordinary. These remarkable individuals all share a common trait: an unwavering commitment to their responsibilities, driven by a call of duty with a strong sense of "why."

The phrase, *call of duty,* embodies a profound obligation to fulfill tasks, missions, or purposes—often involving personal sacrifice and exceeding expectations. Our call of duty is central to competence, demanding consistent effort and growth. While many successful individuals eventually attained greatness and competence, it took time and persistence. Mastery isn't achieved in a single endeavor; it requires overcoming challenges and staying committed to cultivating competence.

Air Jordan – *It Was Never About the Shoe*

When I think of competence, Michael Jordan immediately comes to mind. But the truth is, he wasn't always Air Jordan. Competence isn't natural; it's nurtured. It can only be nurtured when we have clarity about our commitment.

In the movie *Air,* Nike executive Sonny Vaccaro, portrayed by actor Matt Damon, delivers a profound speech that solidifies Jordan's calling. It's a memorable scene.

> *"I'm going to look you in the eyes, and I am going to tell you your future. You were cut from your high school basketball team. You willed your way to the NBA. You ARE going to win championships. It's an American story, and that's why Americans are going to love it.*
>
> *People are going to build you up because when you are great and new, we love you. . . . You are going to change the world. But do you know what? Once they build you as high as they possibly can, they are going to tear you back down. It is the most predictable pattern. . . .*
>
> *I'm going to tell you the truth. You are going to be Attacked. Betrayed. Exposed. Humiliated. And you will survive that. A lot of people can climb that mountain. It's the way down that breaks them! Because that's the moment when you are truly alone.*
>
> *And what will you do then? Can you summon the will to fight on through all the pain? And rise again? Who are you, Michael? That will be the defining question of your life. I think you already know the answer. That's why we are all here.*
>
> *A shoe is just a shoe until somebody steps into it! Then it has a meaning."*[65]

Vaccaro was right. Jordan encountered his fair share of storms in his career. Yet, seventeen years later, you would still find Jordan stepping into his shoes and facing the mountain every night. He played the game with unwavering conviction, resulting in six championships and multiple MVP awards.

My oldest son and I had the privilege of seeing Jordan play. It was a cold night in late December of 2001. At thirty-eight years of age, Jordan was near retirement. But in this game, he was magic as he lifted himself and his team. He may have had only a handful of dunks, but every shot was a thing of beauty. By the end of the night, he would score fifty-one points, leading his team to victory over the Charlotte Hornets.

What you could see in Jordan, whether watching on TV or at the arena, was his unrelenting love for the game, night in and night out. It was a calling—a sense of duty.

> *"My job was to go out there and play the game of basketball as best I can and provide entertainment for everyone who wanted to watch."*[66]

Jordan played with a sense of duty and conviction. What if we approach our pursuits with a fraction of Jordan's dedication and commitment? What kind of impact to you think we could make?

Ready to Leap?

When I think of Michael Jordan, I picture him taking flight—soaring for a dunk. It also brings to mind his home state of North Carolina and what happened at Kitty Hawk at the turn of the twentieth century. This is when Orville and Wilbur Wright made history with the first powered flight. Meanwhile, their sister Katharine, holding down the fort in Ohio, acted as their life coach, providing constant support and encouragement. The Wright Trio turned what was once deemed impossible into reality.[67]

In life, we are faced with two choices:

☐ Sit back and watch the world change, hoping for the best, or

☐ Take a leap of faith and change our world while others watch.

One choice leaves us wondering; the other invites us to trust and actively shape the future. Is faith truly *faith* unless we are willing to leap?

Challenges lie in the potential zone. We may falter, but we can also surpass our expectations. Like Michael Jordan or the Wright Trio, we can learn to fly. Faith pursued builds the grit to carry us forward. It comes down to a call of duty. Do you have one? And if so, do you trust it?

Think of the instinctive duty of a bird. Most birds are meant to fly. But a bird that doesn't leave its nest never discovers its true potential. We are the same.

To guide us in our calling, let's use a preflight checklist similar to what a pilot uses before takeoff. Each item will guide us and give us the confidence we need to further our competence.

Checklist Item #1 – Check Your Values (To Know the Path)

There's a recurring theme across the 3Cs that shouldn't be overlooked. Each of the 3Cs of Resilience, including the commitment to duty that's essential for competence, requires a continual check on values. Keep those values front and center. Without them, fears and doubts can take over.

Values provide the stepping stones we need for vision. They help us know where to put our feet. Without values, we will wander off the path. It's hard to face a mountain without a trail. Values give us the foothold we need.

What are your values? What beliefs and behaviors do you feel you need to leverage? Here are a few to consider:

Tenacious

Means hope pursued. It's about having the resolve to move forward. The only time to pause is when gaining situational awareness and forming a plan. Otherwise, be ready to go. Why? Because when you are tenacious, you are prepared to leap and take flight!

Taking a leap of faith can be scary and leave us feeling vulnerable. Jackie Robinson likely felt this way when he first stepped onto a major league field. Facing resistance can seem irrational, and vulnerability can feel overwhelming. But it's exactly what we need to change our world.

Vulnerability

It comes with fear. But fear isn't what stops us—our response to it does. Experiencing fear is natural before a leap; it signals that we're stepping out of our comfort zone. When aligned with our values, like being intentional, vulnerability becomes a catalyst for growth.

Intentional

Means acting with purpose and clarity. It's about aligning our actions with our core beliefs and values. When intentional, we focus on what matters, taking deliberate steps toward meaningful results. This focus eliminates distractions and keeps us on track.

Courageous

Involves stepping into the unknown, taking risks, and confronting challenges head on. Courage isn't the absence of fear but the willingness to push through it. It empowers us to make tough decisions and persist when the path is difficult, driving innovation and change.

Ultimately, choosing tenacity, vulnerability, intentionality, or courage is a commitment to trust—it's when we surrender our limiting beliefs and finally say, *"Why Not?"*

Trustworthy

Means doing what we say we'll do and being reliable in every situation. Trust is built through consistency and integrity. When we are trustworthy, others know they can count on us, which strengthens relationships and fosters collaboration. Trust is the foundation of leadership and influence, making it one of the most valuable attributes we can develop.

Realignment of trust should happen frequently. It's easy to stray from the path without regular alignment. Once we have our values, we shouldn't overthink—just act! Decisive action is the ultimate measure of trust.

Checklist Item #2 – Check Your Calling (To Stay on Task)

Let's identify our calling in life and our commitment to it.

Teddy Roosevelt, once said that part of our duty is to fight on despite the *"errors* and *shortcomings."* It's about *"daring greatly"* in the face of critics. It's about *"sweating, falling,* and *bleeding."* It's about positioning ourselves to experience *"the triumph of high achievement"* even if we might fail.[68]

Failures and shortcomings are inevitable, but they are where the real learning happens. It's through these experiences that we improve and become competent.

Becoming better means enduring mistakes and staying true to the values we are committed to (see Checklist Item #1). It's how we learn to get back up.

Checklist Item #3 – Check Your Hope (To Get Back Up)

If I had gone to the Air Force or the Naval Academy, as I once dreamed, I would have been introduced sooner to Roosevelt's *The Man in the Arena*. The freshmen at both academies must memorize it—and live it! I see it as an anchor message that reflects the *Face the Mountain* mindset. I only wish I had known of it sooner.

During my last semester of college, I was ready to quit. In hindsight, I wanted to get off the mountain and be a spectator in the arena—not a player. I was tired of school. But then I was reminded of my hope and encountered Roosevelt's speech, which inspired me. In the process, I had to face my inner critic. I had to remind myself that I had hope and a future. That's when I began to dream again. Eventually, a difficult winter turned into a promising spring.

For me, the question, *"You still have hope, don't you?"* pulled me out of my slump all those years ago. It continues to serve as a reminder of life's potential. Success doesn't come to those unwilling to fail; it comes to those who fall and get back up. That's why it never hurts to look for hope.

Checklist Item #4 – Check Your Faith (To Make a Play)

There is a watered-down version of faith commonly in use today, which focuses on what one believes, not on what one does. But Roosevelt implicitly states in *The Man in the Arena* that it's about behavior. The author of the book of James said it well:

> *"Faith without works is dead."*[69]

The word *faith* has changed over the centuries. One definition is that it represents complete trust or confidence in someone or something. I personally like that definition. But today, faith can convey one's religious belief or stance. As in, *What faith are you?* I don't think they are the same, though.

The original word for faith is the Hebrew word *emunah*, which means firmness, fidelity, steadfastness, and steadiness.[70] Faith in this context is about belief, loyalty, and having *"behavior consistent with that stance of trust and reliance."*[71] The people who conduct this kind of faith are the people who work hard to make a play. They put their faith into action again and again.

In the early days, faith (or *Emunah*) was an observable quality of a person. It's what you would look for in a leader, a warrior, or the man or woman in the arena. Like Jordan on the court, it represents someone who perseveres with conviction of belief and who lives with trust and hope. They are making a play.

What if we could bring back this original intent of faith? What impact might it make on our lives if grit was married with our faith?

In Roosevelt's more extensive speech, after the section that became known as *The Man in the Arena*, he shares this thought:

> *"There is need of a sound body, and even more of a sound mind. But above mind and above body stands character . . . good faith and sense of honor."*[72]

Character, good faith, and honor are indicators of resilience. They represent the *Face the Mountain* mindset. But what does he mean by the phrase *good faith*?

In the twenty-first century, *good faith* is used to describe legal matters. People buy something in good faith when they believe they have title to the property being exchanged. Thrown around is the Latin term *bona fides*, which is used to describe good faith negotiations. The phrase *bona fide,* when pronounced in the singular, means someone or something genuine. Faith and grit, as described in this book, are about living with a *bona fide* commitment where our word is our bond.

Roosevelt urges us to do our duty and be in the arena. But being in the arena means facing the critics while committing to duty. Checking our faith gives us the strength to endure and the grit to get back up when we get knocked down. No matter what, we can still make a play. The results of this are called *strength* and *honor.*

Checklist Item #5 – Check Your Grit (To Win the Fight)

Strength and honor brings to mind Maximus from the movie *Gladiator,* standing bloodied in the arena. Commodus, the emperor of Rome, wants him dead.

Earlier, Maximus, had been Rome's heroic general. He led his men to victory and reminded them that, *"What we do in this life echoes in eternity."*[73]

Maximus was all about commitment to duty, and Marcus Aurelius, the Roman emperor at that time he was General was his mentor. What he saw in Maximus was *emunah* type faith and commitment, and he wanted him, not his son Commodus, to succeed him and save Rome from corruption.

But Commodus had other plans, and kills his father to become emperor. He then orders the death of General Maximus, but somehow Maximus escapes death only to end up enslaved.

Even with his title striped away, Maximus represented Roosevelt's qualities: character, good faith, and honor, all things that Commodus lacked.

Maximus's final battle in the arena is against Commodus. Wounded and weakened, Maximus still prevails with resilience and faith, defeating Commodus and freeing Rome before his death. His courage and relentless pursuit of justice are a testament to the power of grit.

Maximus in this story is YOU, but Commodus is your critic. Ask yourself, *"Who is the critic standing in my way?"* Are there naysayers in your life like Commodus saying, *"You can't,"* *"You shouldn't,"* or *"I wouldn't"*? And when you look in the mirror, could one of those critics be you?

Oscar Wilde fittingly once said, *"The critic has to educate the public; the artist has to educate the critic."*[74] Which role do you choose? If you aim to challenge the status quo and inspire change, be the artist, not the critic. Be committed to duty. That's our sign of grit.

Checklist Item #6 – Check Your Work (To Live by The Light)

When Teddy Roosevelt was six years old, he witnessed Abraham Lincoln's funeral procession. Roosevelt admired Lincoln and studied his life closely. Like the character Maximus, Lincoln embodied resilience, character, faith, and honor. Ten presidential terms later, Roosevelt stepped into the exact same arena as Lincoln. He was only forty-three.

One of Roosevelt's favorite quotes from Lincoln was from his second inaugural address.

"Let us strive on to finish the work we are in."[75]

Those eleven words became a mantra for Roosevelt.

History books show how Roosevelt himself became a man of resilience. He was all about service, striving to finish, giving it everything he had. This is what *resilience* meant to him. And maybe for his mentor Lincoln, too:

"I am not bound to win,
but I am bound to be true.
I am not bound to succeed,
but I am bound to live by the light that I have."[76]

◆　◆　◆

Action Steps

We face mountains in multiple areas of life: work, home, school, health, church, commute, and even our calendars or emails. These challenges reveal who we are and where we are.

Our actions tell the world—and ourselves—something about our resolve. Experience builds competence, and faith and grit reflect strength.

Here are six action steps to cultivate competence:

1.　Clarify Your Values

Reflect on your core beliefs and align your actions with them.

2.　Define Your Duties

Duty is more than just a job; it's a commitment. Shift your perspective from *"I have to"* to *"I get to."*

3.　Nurture Your Hope

Hope fuels perseverance. Stay connected with what inspires you. Consider the words from Ritchie Torres who offers this perspective:

"Even in our moment of greatest darkness, there is light. And there is hope. And there is hope not only for our own lives, but we should be hopeful about our ability to change the world."[77]

4. Strengthen Your Faith

Faith, like a muscle, grows stronger with use. Act with confidence even when the outcome is uncertain.

5. Commit to Your Calling

Take steps—big or small—to your calling. Competence grows through effort. As Nike's slogan says, *"Just do it!"*[78]

6. Strive to Endure

Endurance is about committing to the work ahead, even when it's challenging. It also means refusing to let external recognition define your success. Show up daily, focus on the present, and push forward with grit.

To close, reflect on these goals and recommit to pushing forward with determination. This is what it means to commit to duty.

ACT TWO – COURAGE

*"Are YOU going to make the hard but right decision
even if it costs you personally?"*
– Gunny

L ife throws us curveballs. Even a single day can be overwhelming. Yet, we are encouraged to stay diligent in our faith—to be strong and courageous. But in the face of trials, challenges, and fears, where do we find the courage to *dare greatly*?

Courage isn't just a feeling; it's a choice. It's about confronting apprehension and difficulty head-on. When we *face the mountain*, we choose to be courageous; we don't wait to feel brave.

As author and speaker Dave Cornell shares. *"Fear calls us to be spectators. Courage calls us to get in the game."*[79] No battle is ever won without choosing to be courageous; it requires stepping out of our comfort zone and into the potential zone.

In the context of resilience, courage plays a pivotal role. It's the driving force that pushes us forward, even when outcomes are uncertain, or success isn't guaranteed. Resilience requires this courage—not only to confront challenges but also to adapt to changes and keep moving forward. It's the willingness to get back up after a fall and try again, even when the odds seem against us.

By choosing courage, we empower ourselves to persevere, grow stronger, and expand our boundaries.

In the chapters ahead, we'll explore the ABCs of COURAGE to fortify our resilience:

- **Ask, *"Why Not?"*:** Challenging limitations and embracing possibilities.

- **Be Curious:** Letting curiosity drive us beyond fear.

- **Create Calm:** Finding peace amidst chaos to stay grounded.

6 – ASK, *"WHY NOT?"*

*"The man who asks a question is a fool for a minute,
the man who does not ask is a fool for life."*
— Confucius

Have you ever played Capture the Flag? In this outdoor game, two or more teams compete by protecting their flag while trying to steal their opponent's. It's an intense game that combines offense and defense. It's a game symbolic of life.

In pursuit of our dreams, we must move forward to grow while protecting what is important to us. Capturing the flag is about asking, *"Why Not?"*

Gear Up for Battle

Metaphorically, the flag we protect represents our values, whereas the flag that we chase represents our vision. A war is being waged to shake our faith and disrupt our thoughts. The critic seems eager to rob us of our future.

Whether intended or not, the critic's words can plant seeds of doubt that disrupt our faith and distract our attention. Think of all the noise and clutter competing for our attention, questioning our impact, raising fear, and disguising the truth. We should sense the attack when self-doubt starts to creep in. If we don't process it correctly, criticism can feel like little atomic bombs dropping on our brain.

Like a game of Capture the Flag, we need to stay on our toes. It's as if the enemy knows that imagination is our most influential muscle. The critic plays the fickle fan in the crowd, shouting advice we can't afford to hear. The critic is skilled at finding ways to distract us, even when we try to keep our mind in the game.

When it comes to imagination, every distraction is potential exploitation. Our imagination will either lift us or limit us. If we don't guard our thoughts—guard our flag—we risk falling into a dangerous state of vulnerability.

The good news is that faith and grit remind us we are not alone; they build resilience and help us push through opposition. When we align with our values, our imagination reveals what's possible and lights the way. Faith and grit give us the confidence to step onto that path, motivating us to persevere and achieve.

Courage Is a Choice

We often believe courage is a feeling and think we must feel courageous before we do something. However, courage is a choice, not a feeling. The power to ask, *"Why Not?"* is a pivotal step that can propel us toward courage.

"Why Not?" encourages creativity and innovation, challenges assumptions, and fosters a growth mindset. It promotes risk-taking. Additionally, *"Why Not?"* drives progress.

The alternative temptation might be to ask, *"Why?"* But that's a dangerous place. *"Why?"* gives you an excuse not to try. It is limiting and creates the potential for defensiveness. *"Why?"* also stifles creativity and turns our imagination against us. Whereas *"Why Not?"* gives us permission to do something we've never done before.

"Why?" focuses on the past, whereas *"Why Not?"* focuses on the future.

I love asking, *"Why Not?"* because it directs our focus toward what we hope to achieve. When asked with integrity, it positions us to make an impact.

Think about President John F. Kennedy, who, in his inauguration speech, captivated a nation with this one statement:

> *"Ask not what your country can do for you.*
> *Ask what you can do for your country."*[80]

Many Americans are inspired by these words. They challenge us to get out of our comfort zones and lead us to do things that might scare us. They turn courage into a choice.

One year later, in 1962, Kennedy challenged the nation with a *"Why Not?"* vision to go to the moon. In that speech, he shared an intriguing story that propels us to face our mountains by seeing challenges as opportunities.

"Many years ago, the great British explorer George Mallory, who was to die on Mount Everest, was asked why did he want to climb it. He said, 'Because it is there.' Well, space is there, and we're going to climb it, and the moon and the planets are there, and new hopes for knowledge and peace are there."[81]

In 1969, less than seven years after his vision was cast, man successfully landed on the moon, motivated by a *"Why Not?"* question.

A year before that lunar landing, John F. Kennedy's younger brother, Robert F. Kennedy, was speaking at the University of Kansas as he campaigned for the presidency of the United States. In that speech, which was less than three months before RFK's assassination, he shared words that resonate to this day.

Here's a short excerpt of that speech that I have taken the liberty of sorting and shortening. (Note: These are his words, but in a slightly different order.)

"All around us . . . men have lost confidence in themselves, in each other, it is confidence which has sustained us so much in the past.

I want us to find out the promise of the future, what we can accomplish here in the United States, what this country does stand for and what is expected of us in the years ahead.

George Bernard Shaw once wrote, 'Some people see things as they are and say why? I dream things that never were and say, why not?'"[82]

Asking *"Why Not?"* may be the first and most significant step toward courage. Yet, how often do we let opportunities slip through our fingers due to hesitation? How frequently does fear prevent us from approaching a mentor, boss, coworker, friend, or someone we admire?

Failing to ask, *"Why Not?"* throttles our courage. However, the simple intent of asking can be transformative and change everything. Learning to ask sets our intentions and propels us to receive.

The book of James tells us that we do not receive because we do not ask.[83] The foundational element of courage lies in mastering the art of asking, *"Why Not?"*

Wilma Rudolph – *Who Says You Can't?*

I didn't like to read as a kid, but the librarian at my elementary school knew I loved sports and wanted me to discover what I was missing. So, she introduced me to the champion athletes in the library's biography section. They were all back there. I remember meeting Jim Thorpe, Jesse Owens, Frank Gifford, Julius Erving, Jackie Robinson, and more. I couldn't get enough of them in the books that I read, and this passion for reading has stayed with me throughout the years.

One of the books that left an impression on me was the story of Wilma Rudolph.[84] Among all the stories, hers stands out the most. Initially, I was intrigued by Wilma Rudolph because she was an Olympian like Jim Thorpe and Jesse Owens. Nicknamed "Skeeter," she won three gold medals in the 1960 Summer Olympics, earning her the title of "the fastest woman in the world." This included running the 100-meter sprint in eleven seconds flat.

However, what intrigued me the most was learning that, as a child, she was disabled and unable to walk due to the toll of polio, scarlet fever, and double pneumonia. Doctors had told her family that she would need help from her siblings for the rest of her life.

Her mom, though, never lost hope. She believed that Wilma would walk again. It's one of my favorite stories of the "power of asking" related to resilience. It's a story of courage.

When Wilma was six, she found a way to hop on one leg despite her physical challenges. By age eight, she moved around with a leg brace that gave her more mobility. A few years later, at eleven, she discovered the joy of sports, learning to play basketball with her brothers and sisters. Soon, other sports captured her attention. I imagine some of the questions she asked herself, spurred by her mother, were, *"Who says I can't? Why not me? What if I try? Who's to stop me?"*

You can trace this line of questioning from a remark she made when reflecting upon her early life:

> *"After the scarlet fever and the whooping cough, I remember I started to get mad about it all. . . . I went through the stage of asking myself, 'Wilma, what is this existence all about? Is it about being sick all the time? It can't be.' So, I started getting angry about things, fighting back in a new way with a vengeance."*[85]

Don't miss the significance of this story. The challenges you face might be meant to be confronted head-on. The most courageous act isn't asking, *"Why?"*; it's asking, *"Why Not?"* and *"What If?"*

When Wilma turned twelve, sports became her life. By the time she was sixteen, she had miraculously made her way to Melbourne, Australia, as a member of the U.S. Olympic Team and was called upon to run a leg of the 4 x 100-meter relay. She and her team came in third, winning the bronze medal, but that was just the beginning.

Four years later, at barely twenty years old, she returned to the track in Rome, Italy. This time, she won individual gold in the 100 and 200 meters and team gold in the 4 x 100-meter relay. This was the girl who, nine years earlier, was learning how to walk, jump, and run. The three gold medals she won in Italy were all world records.

It's About Courage

After retiring from track in 1962, Wilma Rudolph dedicated herself to coaching and helping underprivileged children. Her calling was to inspire others to understand the power of courage. Through her work, she empowered the next generation, showing them that with courage, they could overcome any obstacle.

Courage is linked to those who seek new worlds and aim to improve themselves and others. However, before you seek, learn to ask.

- *Ask for what you want.*
- *Ask for what is needed.*
- *Ask for what you can do.*
- *Ask for the opportunity.*

Asking gives us a reason to try. When we ask, *"Why Not?"* we position ourselves to seek and make an impact.

Top Benefits of Questions

The best way to find courage is to ask questions. Here are some clear benefits of why we should ask great questions:

1. **To Clarify Purpose**

   Questions help define our intentions and objectives, guiding us toward courageous decisions.

2. **To Overcome Fears**

Fear often holds people back from taking action. Asking questions force us to confront fear head-on, empowering us forward.

3. **To Gain Knowledge**

Questions allows us to gather information and better understand the situation, leading to informed, confident choices.

4. **To Build Connections**

Relationships matter. The right questions can cultivate lifelong connections and relationships that foster collaboration and inspire courage.

5. **To Target Goals**

Asking questions helps us set and focus on specific goals and objectives, creating a clear roadmap for future success.

6. **To Improve Accountability**

When we ask, we hold ourselves accountable; we clarify our intentions in way that can only be measured by courageous action.

7. **To Influence Change**

Courage involves making changes, whether personal or professional. Asking questions signals a readiness for growth and transformation, and initiates a call to action.

8. **To Boost Confidence**

When we ask and receive, our confidence grows, fueling further courageous actions.

9. **To Break Barriers**

Challenging the status quo through questions opens doors to new possibilities.

10. **To Foster Growth**

Courage develops over time through consistent inquiry and action powered by questions. We build a foundation for growth by starting with the courage to ask.

As you reflect on these benefits, remember that asking, *"Why Not?"* is a powerful step toward clarity, overcoming fear, gaining knowledge, connecting, setting goals, improving accountability, influencing change, building confidence, breaking barriers, and fostering growth.

Nelson Mandela – *Unconquerable Courage*

One of my favorite stories about courage and someone who faced the mountain is the story of Nelson Mandela.

As a young man, Mandela dreamed about making a difference in the freedom struggle for South Africans. The apartheid government, determined to eliminate rights for Black South Africans, saw Mandela as a threat. Advocating for change, he was labeled a potential terrorist and imprisoned. In 1964, Mandela was sent to Robben Island, South Africa's version of Alcatraz, where he endured hard labor and harsh conditions. He was confined to a small cell with minimal comforts for eighteen years before being moved to a slightly better prison.[86]

Mandela remained relevant during his imprisonment as a powerful symbol of resistance against apartheid. His imprisonment highlighted the regime's oppression and made him an international icon for justice. Despite being imprisoned, he communicated with supporters through smuggled letters, maintaining his influence and leadership. His leadership in the ANC and advocacy for non-violent resistance had already established his significance. Global support for Mandela and the anti-apartheid movement grew, with international pressure mounting on the South African government.

By the 1980s, it became clear that apartheid was wrong, and discussions of sanctions began to be debated. Mandela's steadfast moral authority and communication with supporters kept his influence alive. However, there were concerns that if the West imposed sanctions, South Africa could (or would) align with the Communist powers. It became clear that the one person who could help lead them was Nelson Mandela, though he was still a political prisoner.

Mandela's refusal to compromise on his principles inspired many, elevating his status as a moral leader. Within South Africa, his imprisonment galvanized the anti-apartheid movement, providing hope and motivation to those fighting the regime. Even Ronald Reagan, the president of the United States, among others, called for Mandela's release, arguing that *"Nelson Mandela should be released to participate in the country's political process."*[87] Four years later, in 1990, Mandela was freed.

Mandela's long imprisonment shaped his character, allowing him to unite people and lead with the 3Cs: Competence, Courage, and Compassion. He once said, *"The greatest glory in living lies not in never falling, but in rising every time we fall."*[88]

This statement sheds light on his convictions. It's what facing the mountain is all about.

How to Be Courageous

Here are four empowering strategies I use to remind me *"Why Not?"*

Strategy #1 – Face Reality

Pressure has a way of forging diamonds. Picture the battle, being inside the arena. Those outside the arena miss the real action. When we step into the arena and ask, *"Why Not?"* we aren't spectators; we are soldiers. Soldiers grow stronger in adversity, recognizing it as a catalyst for growth.

Now, take a moment to reflect on your journey thus far. How have the *"Why Not?"* moments shaped you despite the pressure? What trials and tribulations have you overcome? Consider the growth you've experienced. Has it made you bitter, or has it left you better?

Strategy #2 – Discover Opportunity

Bitterness is often an emotional response to disappointment. It can destroy us if we let it. But what if we viewed challenges differently? Oliver Goldsmith once said, *"In the midst of difficulty lies opportunity."*[89] Recognize the opportunity before us.

We are called to *face the mountain*, and life prepares us for the challenge. The best way to be resilient is to be firm in our faith and ask, *"Why Not?"* Recognize that *needs* create opportunities to succeed, and it is through these challenges that our faith is strengthened. Endurance requires courage.

Courage is about standing firm in faith. How do we get back up when we fall down on the mountain? Remember, there is always something to hope for. Look for the silver lining. *What does your imagination show you? What is the opportunity in the midst of the challenge?*

Strategy #3 – Embrace Imperfection

At times, we might feel undeserving of life's goodness, weighed down by our mistakes. If unchecked, this can breed bitterness and self-criticism, chaining us to regrets. But we can choose to get back up and ask, *"Why Not?"*

We are imperfect beings. Regret can anchor us to the past, leading to a mental replay of *"If only"* or *"Why did I?"* moments that haunt us. According to bestselling author Daniel Pink, 83 percent of people admit that regret has affected them, wishing they had done something differently.

In his book *The Power of Regret,* Pink classifies four categories:

- **Foundation Regrets:** Failures to be responsible or prudent, like neglecting school, overspending, or adopting unhealthy habits. It's when we say, ***"If only I'd done the work."***[90]

- **Boldness Regrets:** Inactions during times when we look back on something we should have taken a chance. It's when we say, ***"If only I'd taken the risk."***[91]

- **Moral Regrets:** Moments of compromised integrity. It's when we say, ***"If only I'd done the right thing."***[92]

- **Connection Regrets:** Not honoring relationships. It's when we say, ***"If only I'd reached out."***[93]

Regret can paralyze us, but faith can create lift. Faith is trusting in something greater than ourselves. For many, that faith is in God. As Charles Spurgeon's said, *"God forgives sinners, not because they are good, but because he is good."*[94] That is a powerful thought about faith.

Imperfections don't define us; they make us genuine. Perfection is overrated—it keeps us from taking action. Courage, however, is about pursuing excellence despite our flaws.[95]

Each of us can be courageous despite our past. When challenges arise—and they will—why not stand up and fight? Like the apostle Paul, we must press on and refuse to dwell on past regrets, because looking back only slows us down.

In Roosevelt's arena, the critic's trick is distraction. As a remedy, the Bible calls us to *"take our stand"* and *"press on"*. Faith and grit allow us to stand confidently despite distractions.[96]

The goal is not just to gain experience but to learn from it. Evaluated experience helps us grow and re-enter the arena. Consider what Coach Herb Brooks told his team before they faced their giants on the ice in the 1980 Winter Olympics,

> *"Great moments are born from great opportunity. You were meant to be here. This is your time. Now go out there and take it."*[97]

Strategy #4 – Choose Grace

Sometimes my computer gets bogged down and slow. When that happens, I just need to give it grace and do a reset. You and I are the same way. We can get overwhelmed by the noise and clutter, losing the ability to process things. Sometimes we're not fully present, or are distracted. That's when we need to give ourselves grace and hit the reset button.

Choosing grace means reflecting on the good around us, and appreciating how fortunate we are. As a place to start, consider the opening words of the Bible, which remind us of the world's creation:

> *"In the beginning God created the heavens and the earth."*[98]

This invites us to reflect on the world's Creation: light, sky, ocean, land, mountains, plants, the moon, the stars, fish, birds, mammals, and humans. A few verses later, it says:

> *"Let [man and woman] have dominion . . . over all the earth."*[99]

Here, *dominion* refers to stewardship—our responsibility to manage and care for the resources entrusted to us, including:

- **Natural Resources:** land, water, air, and wildlife.
- **Human Resources:** people, skills, and knowledge.
- **Economic Resources:** money, investments, and infrastructure.
- **Cultural Resources:** art, literature, and heritage.
- **Technological Resources:** tools and innovations.

Reflecting on the resources we get to manage helps us reset our focus and reinforces our leadership responsibilities. It all starts with grace revealing two key truths.

Truth #1: *Leadership = Stewardship*

Leadership isn't just about guiding others; it's about stewardship—making decisions and taking actions that protect and develop the resources entrusted to us, including people. True leadership preserves and enhances these resources—whether natural, human, economic, cultural, or technological—for the benefit of others and future generations. By embracing our roles as stewards, we honor our responsibilities and contribute to a better world.

King David's example resonates with this idea of stewardship. As king, he was entrusted with the responsibility of an entire nation, starting with one tribe and eventually leading all twelve tribes of Israel. Faced with the mountains before him, David knew he didn't have to climb them alone:

> *"I lift up my eyes to the mountains—where does my help come from? My help comes from the Lord, the Maker of heaven and earth."[100]*

This verse captures the essence of resilience. David relied on his Creator for guidance, recognizing his role as a steward of what had been entrusted to him. We, too, are called to be stewards of the world around us, reflecting on the blessings we have and what we are called to create.

We should ask ourselves: *"What are we speaking life into?"* Consider what the world offers us and what we have to offer in return. Each of us is given a mission to be stewards on this planet, and none of us are here by accident. Our experiences shape who we are and the impact we can make.

We should ask: *"Are we settling for the comfort zone, or are we seeking to make a difference in the potential zone? How far can we climb if we help others climb, too?"*

With this mission of stewardship, what if each of our lives were measured by the 3Cs of Resilience: Competence, Courage, and Compassion? What if this was the measure of our stewardship responsibility?

Courage is at the core of every biblical story, whether it's David facing Goliath, Noah building the ark, or Daniel in the Lion's Den. These were ordinary people who lived with faith and grit, which allowed them to do extraordinary things. Each story reminds us that resilience requires a reset.

The reset involves letting go of what we've been hoarding. If we're not careful, what we hoard can end up owning us more than we own it. But truthfully, we don't own anything; we are stewards.

Are we afraid to let go of the things we think we own because of a fear of missing out (FOMO)? And yet, aren't many of these things of the past? The FOMO we should have, if any, should be asking what opportunities we neglect if we don't live out our calling.

Truth #2: *Letting Go = Potential*

By letting go of what's holding us back, we open ourselves to fully embrace new possibilities and live out our calling with intention; it's how we step into our potential.

Recently, while helping my father-in-law downsize from five storage sheds and a packed house to something more manageable, I realized how much control all that stuff had over his life—and, like secondhand smoke, over the lives of others. In his final months, he recognized it wasn't *things* he needed to steward—it was *relationships*.

This experience caused me to ask: *What am I holding onto that holds me back? What am I really missing out on?*

The right kind of FOMO isn't about clinging to things from the past, but about realizing the potential missed opportunities to live out our future and with the people we care about.

After my landslide fall all those years ago, Hemingway's question is still relevant:

> *"Do you realize that every day forward is now a gift? The question is, what will you do with that gift?"*

There's power in the moment when we see an opportunity to pursue our future. We can either be passive or active. Seeing isn't doing, and it's easy to let excuses get in the way—but that didn't stop Wilma Rudolph. She experienced the right kind of FOMO, which gave her the courage to break free from the shackles of her leg braces. She wanted to experience the joy of running and connecting with others, not sit on the sidelines. It's like the scene from *Forrest Gump* where young Forrest runs as his leg braces holding him back fall away, symbolizing newfound freedom.[101] Wilma experienced that same kind of freedom to step into her potential. We can too!

This reset is about letting go of the comfort zone and stepping into the potential zone. As the apostle Paul reminds us, *"Now faith is confidence in what we hope for and assurance about what we do not see."*[102] It's about trusting the unseen, taking courageous steps toward what's possible, and embracing the unknown to realize our true potential.

Nelson Mandela knew about that kind of faith. He reset his focus even while imprisoned, reading, reflecting, leading fellow inmates. Then, when his shackles came off on his long walk to freedom, he was ready to lead a nation and change the world.

Imagine yourself doing something extraordinary.

Ask, "Why Not?"

Action Steps

This chapter has focused on asking the *"Why Not?"* question—a question that challenges belief, especially when facing challenges. While there may be countless reasons and excuses not to try, remember that the most significant person who can stop you is YOU.

Instead of finding excuses that lead to giving up, look for reasons to try. Ask, *"Why Not Me?"*

Here are six key actions to help you:

1. Challenge Self-Doubt

Confront any hesitation by asking, *"Why Not Me?"* This shifts mindset from doubt to possibility.

2. Seek Opportunities

Instead of dwelling on obstacles, define challenges you care about. Ask yourself questions like *"What's needed?"* and *"What can I do?"* A clearly defined problem gets you halfway to the solution. This approach fosters innovative thinking and effective problem-solving.

3. Embrace the Moment

Don't wait for the perfect moment or condition. Ask, *"Why Not Now?"* to motivate yourself and your team to take immediate action. Courage often requires seizing the present moment.

4. Explore Possibilities

Use *"What if?"* to explore different scenarios and outcomes. This question helps you envision potential successes and challenges, allowing you to prepare and strategize.

5. Take the Next Step

Courage begins with asking the right questions and taking the first step. As Jim Rohn observed, *"Asking is the beginning of receiving."*[103] By shaping your opportunities through asking, you can open doors to new possibilities.[104] It's about combining vision and action to *face the mountain.*

Action without vision wastes time, but when you align both, as Joel Arthur Barker put it, *"Vision with action can change the world."*[105] Start small, ask the right questions, and take decisive action.

6. Find the Reset

The "next step" is critical when climbing the mountain. But sometimes we need a reset. The reset is a combination of all four courage strategies rolled into one: facing reality, discovering opportunity, embracing imperfection, and choosing grace. It's about reflection, assessing your resources, and asking *"Why Not?"*

Think about your reset action plan. Do you have one? It can be a walk on the beach, a trail hike, or a quiet moment by a fire pit. One of my favorite places to reset is the mountains, where I experience clarity and rejuvenation. In those moments free from distractions, I can see the bigger picture and feel ready to *face the mountain.*

Take a moment to capture your thoughts on this lesson. What might be keeping you from asking *"Why Not?"*

7 – BECOME CURIOUS

"Curiosity is the wick in the candle of learning."
—William Arthur Ward

After making the ask, it's time to be bold. Being bold is all about being curious.

I recently observed my son's cat as she quietly stalked the hallway on a mission to discover new worlds. She investigated a bag tucked in the corner, an empty cardboard box in the hall, and even a room that was usually closed but had its door open. The cat explored each of these with unwavering curiosity. A minute later, the cat walked out of the room with a missing cat toy that we thought had been lost. She was happier than a clam.

Life calls us to be curious, and curiosity is the driving force behind discovery. As Bryant McGill wisely stated, *"Curiosity is one of the great secrets of happiness."*[106]

Walt Disney once articulated this sentiment perfectly:

> *"We keep moving forward, opening new doors and doing new things, because we're curious, and curiosity keeps leading us down new paths."*[107]

Disney is absolutely right. The power of curiosity is essential as we *face the mountain* and confront life's challenges. It reveals new paths, and it's what we need to be courageous.

Unlocking Courage – *The Role of Curiosity*

Curiosity is the spark that ignites our courage. This eagerness to discover leads to our greatest achievements. Imagine a world without it—a world where we never ventured beyond the familiar, never sought answers to nature's mysteries, never dared to dream beyond the horizon.

Without curiosity, we wouldn't unlock the secrets of our surroundings, harness the power of fire, or invent the wheel that propels us forward. We wouldn't explore distant lands, build towering monuments, or chart the stars. But we were curious, so we did!

Curiosity didn't stop there. It drove us to unravel the fundamental laws of the universe, from understanding gravity to proving Earth is round. It empowered us to harness the forces of nature, leading to innovations like sailing ships and telecommunications.

Tim Brown, CEO of IDEO, highlights how curiosity plays a crucial role in uncovering unmet needs, often beginning with the question, *"What is missing?"*[108] Curiosity led to groundbreaking discoveries, including penicillin, vaccinations, and the X-ray—revolutionizing healthcare and saving countless lives. It propelled us into the depths of science, unlocking the mysteries of DNA and the cosmos.

From the automobile to the internet, curiosity has been the driving force behind every technological leap that defines our modern world. It propelled us to conquer Everest and place a man on the moon.

But curiosity is more than just a catalyst for change—it's a relentless force undeterred by challenges. It embodies the belief that there is always something more to discover. When paired with faith and grit, curiosity becomes an unstoppable force, driving us to push the boundaries of what's possible.

Curiosity is inseparable from courage. Resilience can't exist without curiosity. Curiosity drives commitment, propels us forward, and helps us rise after being knocked down.

Without curiosity, we lack the foundation for resilience. Without it, our innovation, exploration, motivation, and fortitude are stifled. Courage demands curiosity; it is tied to nearly every pattern of success.

Curiosity introduces risk but also the potential for reward. It calls us to be bold, to venture into the unknown, to seek divine wisdom, to find new ways to overcome challenges, to trust God, and to pursue hope.

Red McDaniel – *Long Suffering Freedom*

In one of my previous books, I shared the powerful story of Captain Red McDaniel, who ejected over the fields of Vietnam after his A-6 aircraft was shot down in 1967.[109] A pilot never wants to ditch his plane, but when you are shot down over enemy territory, tempered curiosity becomes a key to survival. Curiosity always carries a hint of mystery; it can either keep us alive or expose us to danger. The key is to maintain alignment with our calling, values, and training.

For Red McDaniel and his fellow Prisoners of War (POWs), curiosity became a lifeline. It enabled them to find ways to communicate and connect, whether building rapport with their captors or, more importantly, with fellow American prisoners. In recounting his time as a POW, he shared:

> *"It was imperative to communicate in order to know what others were going through in torture so the rest of us could be prepared for the exact kind of questions and the exact kind of torture we were to receive. More than that, we wanted to know from pilots shot down after us how the war was going and, more specifically, any news of our families."*[110]

Curiosity fuels our faith and grit, helping us find ways to never give up. I encourage you to explore more about Red in his captivating book, *Scars and Stripes.*

But let's also recognize the value of curiosity in his story. Red endured nearly seven grueling years as a POW, subjected to brutal beatings, yet he emerged a survivor. Today, he celebrates over fifty years of freedom with his wife in Northern Virginia. Red McDaniel is not just a mentor to me; he embodies the enduring power of faith and grit. He often shares a quote that encapsulates the essence of courage:

> *"Courage isn't the absence of fear; it's the presence of faith."*[111]

This quote perfectly defines courage. When you have faith and grit, you don't eliminate fear, but you greatly reduce it. Curiosity and courage are intertwined: curiosity reflects faith, and courage is the face of grit.

From Red's story, we can identify three benefits of curiosity that allow us to face fear and be courageous.

Benefit #1 – We Discover the Bigger Picture

If you asked Red how he survived, he might tell you about faith, prayer, communication, and determination. In his book *Scars and Stripes*, he offers a profound thought reflecting on his journey: *"Before I could attain the mountaintop, I knew that I must go through the valley."*[112]

When we face death, we think about life. We think about our family, and that triggers a desire to spend time with them. The will to survive is more powerful than any conflict or adversity.

Reflecting on this idea of will, Red recalls the time his father passed away. As a college junior, he returned home to console his mother, who had five younger siblings to care for. He wondered what she was going to do and if he needed to drop out of school. His mother responded simply yet profoundly: *"Where there's a will, there's a way."* Soon after, she found a job and discovered her calling to help others.

Will is a powerful motivator. Will is like a switch that activates our courage; it invites us to be curious and look for a way.

In the words of Victor Hugo, *"People do not lack strength; they lack will."*[113] But when we are curious, it flips on the *"will switch."* Willpower opens doors, and it casts light.

Red shared that *"the brave man is not the man with ice water in his veins; he is, rather, the one who is afraid but still does the job."*[114]

But Red adds that *human will* alone is not enough, *"My human energy and will went as far as it could, but in the end, it was God and God alone who made the difference."*[115]

Because of his faith, Red McDaniel understood the concept of enduring love—a love that remains constant and unwavering despite immense hardship. He experienced firsthand the reality of suffering and isolation, yet he found that the profound truth of God's presence in his life made the pain and loneliness worthwhile. Through his trials, he came to appreciate how this enduring love transcends even the most challenging circumstances.[116]

Benefit #2 – We Act as If We've Been There Before

One thing about Red McDaniel that you should know is that before he fell into enemy hands, he had undergone intense mandatory training to prepare him for that worst-case scenario. He hoped to God that he wouldn't be captured, but his curiosity to learn before taking flight was vital for his future survival.

Ultimately, when he found himself ejecting from his plane and parachuting into Vietnam, he knew he had to adapt quickly to the land. He had to be curious about his options in order to survive. When he was captured sometime later, he also had to keep his composure and act with a calm demeanor as if he had been there before.

A few years back, a clerk at the hotel I was checking into handed me a room key card inscribed with an interesting phrase:

Walk In Like You Own the Place

I remember looking at that key card and thinking, *"This is exactly what I need."* I took it as a sign, and it triggered my curiosity.

Prior to that, I had some apprehension going into the week. The conference was going to be full capacity and full of strangers. I didn't really know anyone. I knew there would be some networking moments, which can be awkward, and there would be a speaker challenge for each of us at our assigned round tables. It was a bit intimidating.

The key card was a resilience reminder that I wasn't alone.[117]

Life is like that. Every day, we face the great unknown. We make connections and first impressions throughout the day.

When we enter a new environment, meet new people, or encounter new opportunities, why not act like we have been there before? Imagine what that would do for our psyche and our resilience.

A catchy jingle for Sure deodorant back in the day echoes this message.

> *"Raise your hand, you got it.*
> *Raise your hand, you know it,*
> *you feel confident, secure.*
> *If you want to feel confident . . . secure . . .*
> *If you want protection . . .*
> *raise your hand and reach for Sure."[118]*

That jingle is silly, I know, but doesn't it describe what resilience should feel like? We need to be ready to reach for faith and grit. It will help us be present and confident.

This *Face the Mountain* mindset offers us the confidence to walk in like we own the place! It reminds me also of a statement from legendary football Coach Vince Lombardi to his players:

> *"When you get into the end zone,*
> *act like you've been there before."[119]*

Lombardi instilled in each of his players a lesson in competence. He conditioned them to be curious and confident.

Benefit #3 – We Can Lead with Confidence

In Act One, we discussed competence, but there's always room for improvement. Curiosity expands our competence by pushing us out of our comfort zone and into the potential zone—where true growth happens. With curiosity as a component of courage, we discover hidden strengths, talents, and capabilities, allowing us to lead with confidence.

Yet even the most competent leaders can struggle with feelings of inferiority. Red McDaniel, for instance, had his confidence shaken during the torture and fear he faced as a POW. In those moments, he wondered how he would survive. But his faith allowed him to reset his confidence, sparking curiosity to know how grit could carry him through. This curiosity expanded his competence and bolstered his confidence.

Competence reflects our skill level, while confidence pertains to our belief in those skills. Ideally, both should work together. Curiosity acts as a catalyst for competence, leading to greater confidence. It's important to recognize that competence alone isn't enough. The world needs leaders who are both competent and confident, and that stems from being curious. Without curiosity, competence diminishes.

I've found that stubbornness inhibits curiosity. Instead of clinging to entrenched positions, what if we approached challenges with an open mind and a willingness to learn? Embracing curiosity could significantly enhance our ability to lead.

Curiosity allows us to transcend our perspectives and better understand others. By seeking to understand before seeking to be understood, we broaden our awareness and enhance our competence. While confidence often has a ceiling, competence knows no bounds and always leaves room for growth.

Curiosity sustains competence and naturally builds confidence. Confidence embodies faith—faith in oneself, faith in the system, and faith in a higher power. It's the belief that we will find a way. With faith and grit, we can navigate almost any challenge not just because of our abilities but because of our capacity to trust. Ultimately, the highest level of faith—faith in God—transcends any ceiling that confidence might have. That's why Level 5 is called transcendental.

Achieving competence and sustaining confidence requires us to put faith and grit into action. This means stepping out of our comfort zone. That's what curiosity is all about.

Step into New Territory

Do you remember our story of Joseph Jacobson? He was sold into slavery by his brothers and taken to a foreign land, yet eventually, he was miraculously reunited with his family—rescuing them from famine. Through his influence, Joseph's family settled in a region called Goshen in Egypt, north of Cairo, the capital city. Over time, Jacob's descendants multiplied and became known in that region as Hebrews—a term that was somewhat derogatory at the time. The Hebrews were laborers and servants—essentially indentured workers—who contributed to working fields and building structures like the great pyramids.

After 400 years—roughly twelve generations—the descendants of Jacob had grown into a vast population. However, they were now under the rule of a very different king than the one Joseph had served centuries earlier. This new Pharaoh saw the Hebrews as a threat and enslaved them, imposing harsh conditions. Eventually, the Hebrews, who preferred to call themselves Israelites, were ready for freedom. Led by Moses, they took a bold stand to find a new land—a land of promise and freedom.

Now picture the Israelites on the move out of Egypt escaping the oppression of slavery and searching for new land. Like characters in the wastelands of *Max Max*—an iconic 80s movie series recently relaunched in 2024—they had been roaming around the desert for forty years.

But Moses has now passed away. Joshua, their newly appointed leader, is feeling the weight of responsibility. He's sweating a bit. Despite years of training and serving as the right-hand man for Moses, he isn't entirely sure he should be *"the guy."*

Joshua knows the Israelites are weary and restless. With Moses gone, they feel deflated. To make matters worse, a daunting river stands between them and their Promised Land. It's the great unknown—filled with new threats and potential enemies. Like Tom Hemmingway, Joshua is grappling with Imposter Syndrome.

Sensing Joshua's nerves, God, like Gunny, speaks directly to him.

"I will be with you as I was with Moses.
I will NOT fail you or abandon you.
Be strong and courageous,
for YOU are the one who will lead these people.[120]

Be strong and very courageous.
Be careful to obey all the instructions Moses gave you.
Then you will be successful in everything you do.[121]

Be strong and courageous!
Do not be afraid or discouraged.
For the Lord your God is with you wherever you go."[122]

Think about this text. If God emphasized to you three times to be strong and courageous and that success awaits you, wouldn't you be curious about what lies ahead? You'd want to open that door, wouldn't you?

After this divine coaching session from God, Joshua wasted no time rallying his team. He instructed them to *"walk in like they own the place"*—or at least close to it.

"Go through the camp and tell the people to get their provisions ready. In three days, you will cross the Jordan River and take possession of the land the Lord your God is giving you."[123]

Now, keep in mind that this is the newly minted CEO of the Israelites, Joshua. The way I see it, Joshua, who was apprehensive before God's one-on-one, now acts like he's been there before, and they all respond positively.

Rather than doubting him, they say, *"We will do whatever you command us, and we will go wherever you send us."*[124] Now, that's a vote of confidence.

This response reveals something important about people—they want to be led and led well. Joshua had a plan, and they were ready to march to it. Part of that plan was crossing the mighty Jordan River at high tide with the Ark of the Covenant that they were trying to keep from the Nazis. (I might be blending stories.)

The bottom line is that they were curious. *Why?* Because they operated with faith and grit. Resilience calls us to be curious!

Anthropologist and author Angeles Arrien offers this advice:

> *"We must shift our allegiances from fear to curiosity, from attachment to letting go,*
> *from control to trust, and*
> *from entitlement to humility."*[125]

God told Joshua to be strong and courageous three times. That's enough to inspire a little courageous trust and curiosity, don't you think?

What if the same courageous trust and curiosity that inspired Joshua before he took the Promised Land is being offered to you and me? What if we are called to step into new territory?

Resilience in the Face of Adversity

The *Face the Mountain* mindset equips us to be confident in the steps we take. *Why?* Because faith and grit remind us that we are not alone. The apostle Paul shares it this way:

> *"We are hard pressed on every side, but not crushed;*
> *We are perplexed, but not in despair;*
> *We are persecuted, but not abandoned;*
> *We are struck down, but not destroyed."*[126]

This text sounds like a script from a modern-day action movie, doesn't it? Just substitute the phrase *"we are"* with Ethan Hunt, Indiana Jones, or maybe even your own name.

The good news is, there is truth in this statement. Despite all the challenges we face, we are not crushed, likely not in despair, not abandoned, and, since you are reading this with me, clearly not destroyed!

But what if we do feel abandoned? What if we feel like Red McDaniel behind enemy lines? Here are eight survival steps to reframe our thinking.

1. **Acknowledge our feelings**: Recognize and accept our emotions. It's okay to feel abandoned; acknowledging your feelings is the first step toward addressing them.

2. **Reach out for support**: Talk to a trusted person about what you're feeling. This could be a friend, family member, or coach. Sharing these feelings can alleviate the sense of abandonment and provide perspective.

3. **Reflect on the situation**: Take some time to reflect on why you feel abandoned. Is there a specific event or circumstance that triggered these feelings? Understanding the root cause can help us gain clarity and perspective.

4. **Challenge negative thoughts**: Negative thoughts and beliefs can exacerbate feelings of abandonment. Challenge these thoughts by questioning their validity and replacing them with more positive and realistic perspectives.

5. **Practice self-compassion**: Be kind to yourself during a challenging time. Engage in self-care activities that help you feel nurtured and supported, such as exercise, meditation, or hobbies.

6. **Focus on what you control**: While we may not be able to change certain aspects of our situation, focus on what you can control. Set small, achievable goals and take proactive steps toward them.

7. **Seek new connections**: If you feel abandoned by specific individuals, try cultivating new connections and relationships. Join clubs, groups, or communities with shared interests to meet new people and build supportive relationships.

8. **Seek guidance when needed**: If feelings of abandonment persist and significantly impact well-being, seeking support from a therapist or counselor can be beneficial. They can offer personalized strategies to help navigate our emotions and rethink our situation.

Remember, feeling abandoned is a temporary state; with time and support, we can find ways to cope and move forward. Be patient and take things one step at a time. Choose to see yourself not as abandoned, but as a pioneer preparing the way for others. Remember, you are a leader.

Explore the Promises

At this point in the journey, we already possess two of the 3Cs: Competence and Courage. We are ready to *face the mountain*, but being curious about God's promises can 10X our resilience.

One simple exercise is to search for the phrase "God will" in the Bible. This reveals over one hundred passages highlighting the impact of faith and grit when we know we are not alone. Many cast a light of hope and promise across all five Levels of Belief. Here are just a few:[127]

"God Will" Promises

1. "God will provide."[128]
2. "God will fight for you."[129]
3. "God will bless you in all your work."[130]
4. "God will be with you wherever you go."[131]
5. "God will deliver."[132]
6. "God will redeem me."[133]
7. "God will stand with me."[134]
8. "God will help me."[135]
9. "God will hear me."[136]
10. "God will intervene."[137]
11. "God will give you the right words at the right time."[138]
12. "God will never fail."[139]
13. "God will reward you."[140]
14. "God will do whatever you ask."[141]
15. "God will give us many opportunities to speak."[142]
16. "God will meet all your needs."[143]
17. "God will answer your prayers."[144]
18. "God will wipe away every tear."[145]

These promises of hope are profound when tied to prayer. They offer us confidence when we are called to be curious. Like Joshua, a *Face the Mountain* mindset means we never go it alone.

Curiosity Assessment

Where do you stand on the scale of curiosity? Is this a strength you possess in abundance, or is it more subdued? Is it a high, or is it a low?

Think back to your pursuits. How has curiosity shaped you and served you? What discoveries have you made because of it? The power of curiosity expands our knowledge, as reflected in scripture:

> *"Tune your ears to wisdom, and*
> *concentrate on understanding.*
> *Cry out for insight, and ask for understanding.*
> *Search for them as you would for silver;*
> *seek them like hidden treasures."*[146]

Furthermore, curiosity encourages us to ask good questions. These questions, in turn, build trust:

> *"Keep on asking, and you will receive what you ask for.*
> *Keep on seeking, and you will find.*
> *Keep on knocking, and the door will be opened to you.*
> *For everyone who asks, receives.*
> *Everyone who seeks, finds.*
> *And to everyone who knocks,*
> *the door will be opened."*[147]

The message is clear. Ask. Seek. Knock.

Action Steps

This chapter has focused on the importance of curiosity. Curiosity leads to commitment. It allows us to walk into the room as if we own the place. It gives us the strength to *face the mountain,* knowing we won't be crushed, destroyed, or abandoned. With curiosity, we discover that the universe is for us, not against us.

Here are some action steps to cultivate curiosity:

1. Question Assumptions

Challenge your existing beliefs and habits. Ask yourself if they are still serving you or if they need to be re-evaluated. This openness to change can foster a more curious mindset.

2. Seek New Experiences

Have you allowed any old habits or biases to get in the way of curious living? Take steps to actively pursue new experiences and knowledge. Whether it's reading a new book, exploring a new hobby, or meeting new people, stepping out of your comfort zone can ignite curiosity.

3. Reflect on Your Faith and Grit

Faith and grit represent belief and determination. Reflect on how they have helped you overcome challenges in the past. How can faith and grit guide you in approaching new challenges, leading to personal or professional growth?

4. *Review Promises and Commitments*

Are you actively fostering curiosity and seeking to discover new things? Reflect on the "God Will" promises mentioned in this chapter. Identify ways to "test" these promises in your life, using them as a foundation for curious exploration and growth.

5. *Make a Commitment*

Decide on one concrete action that demonstrates your curiosity and commitment to growth. This could be a new project, a learning goal, or a personal challenge. What doors are you presently knocking on? Commit to curiosity and observe how this fosters strength and courage.

Take a moment to capture your thoughts on this lesson in your companion journal. Let curiosity add wind to your sails, guiding you toward the Promised Land.

8 – CREATE CALM

"You can't calm the storm, so stop trying.
What you can do is calm yourself.
The storm will pass."
— Timber Hawkeye

The commitment that stems from being curious needs one more foundational element for Courage to flourish: calmness. When stepping into something you've never done before, making decisions from a place of calm is essential. Think about how Joshua led the Israelites after taking command. He wasn't just strong and courageous—he was calm.[148]

The Calm Question

Deciding to do something isn't the same as actually doing it. Courage starts by asking, *"Why Not?"* and then calmly taking action. Another question might be *"What If?"* but sometimes that's not enough. It can keep you in the "dream" state rather than the "do" state. To move forward, try following *"What If?"* with *"Why Not?"* But before you go do, also ask, *"How will I show up?"* That gets you to calm. I call this the Calm Question.

Let's unpack this further. The challenges you face during a decision can lead to fear and apprehension. If you choose ahead of time how you will be present, you can better *face the mountain.*

Think of the alternative: if we don't ask the right questions, our inner critic will bring a salvo of its own questions that will throw us off. Here are some examples:

- *"What if I can't?"*
- *"What if I don't have what it takes?"*
- *"What if I fail?"*

The counter punch for the inner critic is calmness. One question to ask ourselves that quiets the critic is,

- *"How will I show up?"*

Calmness is a choice available to everyone, but it requires effort to reach hard for that figurative switch—to make the decision and act on it.

I remember my track coach instilling the importance of being calm before the gun sounded in a race. Was I nervous? Absolutely! But I eventually learned to override those nerves by focusing on calmness. My routine was to reflect on a Bible verse that steadied me: *"I can do all things through Christ who strengthens me."*[149]

I recited that verse as a prayer each time I placed my fingers on the starting line. It became a habit and shaped how I showed up. Then, when the gun went off, I left the critic in the dust.

Each of us faces challenges, chaos, and struggles. In such moments, we're faced with two choices:

- to react with emotion, anxiety, and fear, or

- to keep our cool.

We need to find the throttle that leverages faith and grit. Looking back, my best days were when I kept my cool.

Anxiety is a universal human experience that can be debilitating. It can lead to feelings of weakness and mental paralysis. It steals courage, hinders competence, and can render people ineffective. However, if we recognize that calmness is a conscious choice any of us can make, young or old, then we can manage our fear, settle our doubt, and even influence our circumstances. Each of us has the power to create calm despite the chaos around us. But it starts with deliberate awareness.

Awareness Gut Check

A gut check is an evaluation of our "resolve, commitment, or priorities" typically with respect to a course of action.[150] It reveals if we are persevering, spectating, or merely critiquing—a reminder to step into the arena, where true resilience is tested, rather than staying on the sidelines.

Marianne Williamson once remarked, *"Every decision you make reflects your evaluation of who you are."*[151] This is worth contemplating. Our choices aren't just practical or situational; they're deeply connected to our self-perception and identity. The decisions we make reflect how we see ourselves, what we believe in, and what we prioritize. In essence, our decisions serve as a mirror of our innermost thoughts, values, and character.

Now and then, I take a little break, grab a PS4 controller, and play a video game like *Call of Duty*. In most games you can pause mid-challenge—unless you're in a multiplayer campaign. In those cases, players who pause the game and leave teammates stranded aren't typically well-liked. In a multiplayer game, we count on each other's contributions for success.

My friend Daniel compares it to a hockey player checking into a penalty box to take a phone call: *"Hey buddy, we have a match we are trying to win here!"* You don't want to be the one pausing the game and leaving others stranded. If you're gone too long, the server kicks you off. We need to be there to help fight the battle.

Real life is like that. There's no long pause in the midst of a challenge. The game clock of life keeps moving. And it's multiplayer. Often, we fail to realize how equipped we are to persevere, and resilience can be what keeps others going. Keeping calm is crucial.

Some of the best examples of this are found in the journeys of epic mountain climbs. In her book *On the Edge: Leadership Lessons from Mount Everest and Other Extreme Environments*, mountaineer Alison Levine discusses the importance of collaboration and staying calm: *"Some of the world's most talented climbers have lost their lives because they let down their guard."*[152] She adds, *"Teamwork is about looking out for one another, helping one another, and winning together."*[153]

Think back to the choices you've made. Have you ever grown timid or let your guard down? Most of us have, but the key is to learn from those moments. We can improve! The most vital quality in leadership isn't skill or strength—it's our attitude and approach. How can we show up more present and resilient?

Every decision and behavior has shaped who we are today. But think of the impact that we can still make with our attitude, especially when facing the mountain with others.

If you want to measure your leadership resilience, assess your demeanor as a sherpa would. Like Joshua taking the Israelites into the Promised Land or Alison Levine guiding her team to the Everest's summit, how would others rate your level of calm? How did your attitude make a difference for them?

This reminds me of a moment when my dad calmed the storm—at least for me.

Trapped in the Mountain

When I was a boy, my parents thought I was fearless. To them, curiosity should have been my middle name. We lived on the fourth floor of an apartment building in Rio de Janeiro, Brazil. It was located at the base of the foothills of Corcovado, where the Christ the Redeemer statue stands. Nearby was a botanical garden called Jardim Botânico.

I loved where we lived. It was an amazing place to explore. I'd climb rocks, trees, and occasionally get myself into trouble. Despite my bravado, fear followed me. I just did a good job of hiding it—until the day a sudden storm triggered a landslide that buried us in a tunnel.

It was a summer afternoon and Dad took our family to a beach on the other side of Guanabara Bay called the Praia de São Francisco. While my brother and I we were playing in the sand kicking the ball, a storm suddenly appeared on the horizon. It looked haunting. Seeing the threat, my family quickly packed up to leave, hoping to avoid getting caught in a flash flood.

I remember the rain pouring down hard as we crossed a long bridge over part of the bay. The road surface was barely drivable. Then we found some relief from the downpour inside the Rebouças Tunnel (*Túnel Rebouças*), which cut through a small mountain called Elephant Mountain that was on the way to our apartment. But halfway through one of the long stretches of tunnel; the traffic came to a sudden stop.

Minutes passed without movement. Drivers began getting antsy. Soon, people started getting out of their vehicles. I remember Dad stepping out to find out what was going on as we sat in the dark tunnel.

I recall the damp smell and the drab concrete walls and the long shadows cast by the car headlights as people gathered outside their car. It was eerie. Something was clearly wrong.

A few minutes later, Dad returned to the car to fill us in. *"Well, we're not going anywhere anytime soon. There was a mudslide on the other end, and the tunnel is blocked."* We all gasped. That's when the panic set in for me. *We were trapped!*

Someone in the car—maybe it was me—asked, *"Is there no way out?"* My dad, who was super calm, replied. *"Not yet, but there will be. Let's just have faith. The good news is we are safe. And that's all that matters."* He then went back out to strategize a plan with some of the Brazilian motorists. My mom suggested we pray, which helped, but I was still terrified.

Eventually, Dad came back with a plan. The adjacent tunnel, meant for traffic going the other way, was only partially blocked. The idea was to funnel cars to a cross path behind us that connected the two tunnels. Even with that plan, I still felt trapped, with cars everywhere. My brother whispered, *"Hey! We're going to be okay!"*

After what seemed like forever, we turned around and head to the cross path escaped through the alternate tunnel. I was relieved. As we drove out of the mountain, we saw normally busy streets that looked like rivers, and the effects of floodwaters that had pushed cars off the road. Other than the lights of cars, the city was unusually dark.

Years later, I learned that late day scare in 1971 killed 130 people. I couldn't help but wonder, *What would have happened if we left five minutes sooner? Would we have survived?* But what stays with me is the calm leadership of my dad. His steady demeanor kept us safe, allowing him to think clearly and take action. I now realize what trapped me wasn't just the mudslide—it was my own fear. Fortunately, cooler heads prevailed. Calm is a choice.

Understanding Anxiety

Anxiety is a human emotion characterized by feelings of uneasiness, worry, fear, or nervousness. It's triggered when we feel threatened or stressed or encounter a situation beyond our control. Like being stuck in a tunnel with no easy way out. Anxiety can affect us physically, mentally, and even socially. It can be the worst feeling in the world, but we experience it differently.

When we encounter something threatening or feel anxious, our brain kicks into high gear to assess the level of danger. The process begins with a signal from the amygdala, a small region of the brain responsible for detecting fear, which then alerts the hypothalamus to develop a response plan. This plan is carried out by neurotransmitters like norepinephrine, which enhances alertness and sharpens our focus, and serotonin, which influences our mood and emotional state, helping us prepare mentally for the next steps.

The three most typical responses to perceived threats are fight, flight, or freeze.

- Fight occurs when the amygdala, a part of the brain involved in emotional processing, triggers a response to confront the threat aggressively.

- Flight involves fleeing from danger to seek safety.

- Freeze occurs when the amygdala initiates a response of immobility or temporary shutdown in the face of overwhelming fear or danger.

Consider the strategies shared in the next section to foster calm and courage. However, if anxiety is a frequent experience for you, I encourage you to seek outside help. Options include working with a brain health coach or counselor or exploring medical treatments. None of us have to feel alone.

The key thing to remember is that calmness is a choice, and with practice, it can help us withstand almost any storm.

David and Goliath

One example of calm that stands out is the story of David taking down the mighty Goliath. Imagine the situation: Goliath, a giant Philistine warrior, had struck fear into the Israelite soldiers and caused panic throughout the city. If social media like X (formerly Twitter) existed back then, it would likely have been trending with video clips highlighting the terror.

Despite that chaos, David answered the call. A young shepherd in his early teens, long before he became king, David volunteered to confront Goliath. As proof of his credentials, he shared his past experience defending his sheep against wild animals, including a lion and a bear. With faith and confidence, David rejected the bulky armor they wanted him to wear, and chose only five smooth stones and a sling, believing that God would grant him victory and the grit to get it done.[154] This is an example of Level 5 faith and grit. And yet, before he was king, David was seen as a person just like you and me.

Malcolm Gladwell, in his book *David and Goliath*, reframes this story to illustrate that what often appears as a disadvantage can be a hidden strength. David's perceived weaknesses—his youth, size, and unconventional weapon—were actually significant advantages that led to his triumph over Goliath. Gladwell's insight is that challenges and obstacles, like those David faced, often provide unexpected advantages and opportunities for innovation and success.[155] David's victory serves as a reminder that even in the face of formidable odds, hidden strengths can lead to unexpected outcomes. The key is to remain calm.

Jesus and the Storm

Jesus demonstrated this same calmness multiple times. On one occasion, he and his disciples were crossing the Sea of Galilee, and he took a little snooze. While he napped, the weather suddenly got bad, like it did for me and my family in Brazil. The radar picture, if they had iPhones and cell phone coverage to see it, would not have been good. As the storm kicked into gear, they panicked and woke up Jesus, who was still sleeping.

Despite the chaos, Jesus remained calm. Why? Because calm was his default. He calmed the seas, and then turned to his friends and asked, *"You of little faith, why are you so afraid?"*[156]

His question reminds me of the David and Goliath story we just discussed. Unlike the disciples in that moment, David had faith greater than his fear. What if you and I had the same kind of resolve? Jesus suggests that this level of faith is available to us—that we are more resilient than we realize.

Faith is a precursor to resilience, and grit helps us weather the storms. We need both. But why does our faith sometimes seem too small, limiting our grit?

The Brain Rewired

"Little faith," as Jesus described it, reflects a mental state of weakness. Often, when a storm is upon us, we panic—crying out for help or freezing in fear. But what if calm became our default response?

I think back to my dad. He didn't panic in that Brazilian tunnel. He kept his cool, and we all got out safely. Calmness can be cultivated; it's a nurtured response.

Consider the disciples waking up Jesus in a panic during the storm. While they couldn't calm the storm itself, they certainly could have calmed their response to the storm. Imagine if Jesus had woken up not to their panic, but to calmness. Seeing them in control, he might have said something very different: *"You of strong faith. You have let your hearts be calm. With faith, fear has no sting."*[157]

"Fear Has No Sting." Those four words are powerful—and they can be true.

Fear begins in the mind—in the imagination—but quickly sends shockwaves throughout the body. The brain, unable to distinguish between real and imagined threats, triggers the fight-or-flight response. When the amygdala senses fear, it signals the nervous system, causing the release of stress hormones like cortisol and adrenaline. These hormones prepare the body for action by raising heart rate and blood pressure, creating a state of physical readiness or tension that mirrors the perceived danger. Blood flow quickly shifts from our heart to our limbs, feet, and hands, preparing us to either flee or fight.[158]

However, when calm becomes our default, the brain is rewired to counter this automatic response. Regularly practicing calmness through mindfulness, deep breathing, or cognitive reframing strengthens neural pathways associated with relaxation and self-control. Over time, the brain's response to perceived threats changes. The prefrontal cortex, responsible for decision-making and rational thought, becomes more engaged, and the amygdala, the brain's alarm system, becomes less reactive. This rewiring process reduces the intensity of the fight-or-flight response, allowing you to approach challenges with a clear mind and steady heart.

Key Strategies to Remain Calm

When severe storms come, a common reaction is to panic—just think about how quickly grocery stores sell out of bread, milk, and toilet paper. Calm is rarely the default. If you want to see panic in action, turn on the television or check Twitter (now X) during a major news event. Calm is rarely on display. What you'll notice is social panic, not calm. But what if calm became our default? How differently would our world look and behave?

Here are four keys to help us create calm.

Key #1 – Take a Breath

Start with conscious, controlled breathing. It's the quickest way to create calm. Controlled breathing means drawing in a deep breath, slowly blowing out the air, and then breathing in another long breath. Repeat this for up to a minute. Deep breathing through the nose helps as well. This technique is known as the relaxation response.

Studies show that breath awareness is one of the most effective and accessible tools for calming the nervous system.[159] If we sense fear but respond with controlled breathing, our amygdala settles, and our parasympathetic nervous system can kick into gear doing what it does best: decrease respiration and heart rate and increase digestion.

Key #2 – Label Your Emotion

Another powerful technique is labeling our emotions. This simple step of naming our emotions in the midst of fear shifts brain activity from the amygdala to the prefrontal cortex. In my book *IMAGINE*, we focus on a technique called the OODA loop, which stands for Observe, Orient, Decide, and Act.

Observing emotions without become attached to them can be transformative. Start by simply observing what you feel or sense. Rather than react, REFLECT. Be curious about *what* you feel. Just identify and label the fear or anxiety without judgment.

To help, refer to the common emotions listed in Table 2. By labeling the emotion, you may find that it loses its power, making it easier to manage.

Table 2 – Common FEAR/ANXIETY Emotions

Alone	Empty	Lost	Ticked
Anger	Exhausted	Miserable	Tired
Apathy	Fatigued	Nervous	Unfulfilled
Beaten	Frustrated	Petrified	Unmotivated
Bewildered	Guilty	Rejected	Unqualified
Concerned	Hostile	Resourceless	Upset
Confused	Horror	Saddened	Weary
Disappointed	Hopeless	Shocked	Weak
Discouraged	Indifferent	Stressed	Worried
Doubt	Jaded	Surprised	Zapped

Key #3 – Write it Out

Throughout this book, I emphasize the power of words. The written word is compelling. When you feel discouraged or saddened, take a pen to paper and write out that feeling. However, rather than writing from a victim-like mindset, write the letter as if a future version of you is writing to your present self.

To start, use a prompt like, *"I know you are feeling. . . ."* Then, fill in the blank. Here's an example of something I wrote recently using this prompt. Writing it down helped defuse the fear and anxiety I felt and put my foot on a better path.

> *Dear Paul,*
>
> *Right now, you are feeling empty and tired, and you are worried about the next steps in front of you, including those in your care. But I want to encourage you. You've been through this before. This is just a season with some storms. Remember to keep your cool. Your family needs to see that calm demeanor. You need to see it.*
>
> *Look past the current obstacles and set your eye on the prize. Live your values. There are good things ahead for you. Remember, there is no effort that doesn't come without errors and shortcoming. It's part of the journey. Progress is made only when you keep moving. One day, you will look back at all this and see that you were never alone. You got this! Write your story.*
>
> *— Paul*

Key #4 – Let That Stuff Go!

One saying that helps me reset is, *"Let that Stuff Go!"* A variant of this phrase the *S* might stand for something else, which also works. But *Stuff* works for me. This is the fourth tool in the arsenal to create calm and may even have biblical merits.

There is wisdom in letting go of the past and not dwelling on it.[160] For those who live in deep faith, the Bible offers powerful advice: *"Cast all your anxiety on him (God) because he cares for you."*[161] To cast means to throw it away. In other words, *"Let That Stuff Go!"* Hand over our worries and concerns, and let God handle it. Jesus asks a profound question: *"Can any one of you by worrying add a single hour to your life?"*[162]

It's a great question, isn't it?

You and I are not meant to hoard things that hold us back or carry the burdens of fear and worry. These things weigh on us or stress us out. They make it hard to move forward and make an impact. They take joy out of life.

As a symbolic way to *"Let That Stuff Go,"* write the things weighing you down. Then, find someone to help you bear the burden. Like Frodo in *The Lord of the Rings*, we need to cast the ring into the fire, but we also need others to help us get there. The goal is to release it and move on. One suggestion is to (carefully) burn what you wrote, letting it serve as a symbolic gesture of letting go. Afterward, focus on moving forward and shaping a better tomorrow.

Joe Montana - *Cool Under Pressure*

I want to share one more story that reflects the power of calm when we *face the mountain*. In Super Bowl XXIII, quarterback Joe Montana and his 49ers had just three minutes to come back from a ten-point deficit against the Cincinnati Bengals.

Most players would be anxious, and under that kind of pressure, mistakes are easy to make. But Joe Montana earned his nickname "Joe Cool" for a reason. In the huddle, he was calm and confident. To break the tension, he glanced toward the end zone and spotted actor John Candy in the stands. Smiling, he casually said, *"Hey! There's John Candy!"*

His teammates, who had been tense and nervous, looked downfield, and sure enough, there was the celebrity visible in the stands. They turned to Joe and laughed. *"Oh yeah, that is John Candy! Look at that,"* someone said. Joe smiled again, adding, *"Well, that's cool. Now, let's have some fun and go win this game."*

With that, he took command of his team and calmly led them down the field twice to win the game before time expired.[163]

Often, the best way to be courageous and *face the mountain* is to be calm. Calm is contagious—and calm is courageous.

◆　◆　◆

Action Steps

This chapter focused on something within our control: our level of calm. By training our brain to default to calmness, we build resilience. We learn to navigate life's storms with confidence and grace, proving that with faith, fear truly has no sting.

Make calm your default.[164] When we are calm, it's easier to acclimate, stay curious, and walk into the room like we own the place. Furthermore, maintaining calm allows you to become the thermostat in the room—setting the tone for everyone around you. Calm is contagious, and others will naturally mirror the leader's attitude and demeanor.[165]

Here are four action steps—centered on this awareness gut check—that can cultivate calm in a crisis moment:

1. Take a Breath

The first step is to slow down and take a deep breath. Begin by checking in with yourself. Breathing deeply helps reduce stress and brings your focus to the present moment.

2. Label Your Emotion

Recognize how you feel—whether tense or relaxed. Identify and name the emotion you are experiencing. This simple act of labeling can help you gain control over your feelings and reduce their intensity.

3. Write It Out

Take a moment to jot down your thoughts and feelings. Writing can be a therapeutic way to process emotions and gain clarity. This process can provide a release for overwhelming emotions.

4. Let That Stuff Go

Release the tension and let go of negative emotions. Whether it's through a physical gesture, such as shaking your hands out, or a mental release, like visualizing the stress leaving your body, find a way to let it go.

Think about how you can reflect a calm demeanor. Recognize that your level of calm influences those around you. If you are anxious, others will likely be anxious, too. But if you are calm, others will reciprocate the calm.

How will you practice these steps today to reflect calm in your leadership?

ACT THREE – Compassion

*"Do YOU care as much about me and these guys as
YOU care about yourself?"*
— *Gunny*

C ompassion may be the most underrated quality of leadership. It is the ability to empathize with others who may be struggling with their own mountains and offer support and guidance. It involves showing kindness, care, and a willingness to help, often prioritizing others' needs above our own.

When coupled with Competence and Courage, Compassion becomes a powerful differentiator, creating a balanced approach to resilience.

As Zig Ziglar wisely emphasized, *"You can have everything in life you want if you help other people get what they want."*[166] His message underscores the act of giving, highlighting the transformative power of Compassion. It's about embracing a mindset of service and recognizing that our own resilience is often strengthened when we support others in their struggles.

In the context of resilience, compassion plays a dual role. Self-compassion helps us deal with setbacks without harsh self-criticism, allowing us to view failures as opportunities for growth rather than definitive endings. Compassion for others, on the other hand, fosters a support network that provides emotional encouragement and strength during tough times. This sense of connection reduces feelings of isolation and reinforces our ability to bounce back.

Facing the mountain requires us to embody compassion, both toward ourselves and others. No one should ever climb the mountain alone. I learned that lesson multiple times; climbing alone can lead to a landslide. Compassion means we don't just focus on our own journey; we make sure that others are not climbing alone either.

In the final few chapters, we will explore the ABCDs of COMPASSION, which move us from success to significance.

- **Acclimate:** Adjusting to others' needs and environments.

- **Be Intentional:** Taking deliberate steps to show empathy and care.

- **Cultivate Care:** Nurturing kindness towards yourself and others.

- **Do It Anyway:** Putting compassion into action through service and support.

Let's discover how these empower us to not only face our own mountains but also support others in their climb. There may be nothing more significant than that.

9 — ACCLIMATE

E mbarking on a mountain expedition, like Everest, requires a sherpa—an experienced mountaineer who serves as a guide. Their extensive knowledge of the landscape and proficiency make them invaluable, particularly in helping climbers acclimate to high altitudes.

Acclimating is crucial for survival. As you ascend, you must adapt to reduced oxygen levels, lower air pressure, temperature fluctuations, and high winds. Without proper acclimation, the risks increase significantly. Similarly, on our journey in life, adapting to new challenges and changes is essential to success and growth.

Imagine yourself in the boots of a sherpa. They not only help others *face the mountain* but also confront it themselves. Sherpas exemplify compassion and readiness. They are ready to guide and support those in their care. In this chapter, we will explore how we can embody the role of an effective sherpa, learning to adapt and support others.

Dick Hoyt – *Father. Runner. Sherpa*

One of the most inspiring stories of a person who was a sherpa for someone else is the story of Dick Hoyt. After his son Rick was born with cerebral palsy, doctors suggested institutional care, but Dick and his wife, Judy, refused. They raised Rick like any other child despite his quadriplegia.

As Rick grew older, his interest in sports blossomed. At 15, he asked his father to push his wheelchair in a race. This would spark an incredible journey. After that race, Rick told his father, *"Dad, when I'm running, it feels like I'm not handicapped."*[167]

Together, as Team Hoyt, they competed in 1,130 endurance events, including six Ironman Triathlons, seventy-two marathons, and a 3,735-mile cross-country trek. Their favorite race was the Boston Marathon, which they competed in thirty-two times.

Rick was once asked, if he could give his father anything, what would it be? He responded, *"The thing I'd most like is for my dad to sit in the chair and I would push him for once."*[168]

Their story demonstrates resilience and the unbreakable bond between father and son. Dick said, *"If Rick could do it and keep me doing it right alongside him for thirty years, then anything is possible."*[169]

Rick once wrote to his father, *"I hope that everyone who hears our story knows that you taught me the key to my daily life is that I believe the phrase, Yes You Can!"*[170]

This story resonates deeply with me. Just weeks before my landslide fall on The Hook, I helped push a paraplegic teen in a 10K race. The joy of helping someone achieve a dream they thought was impossible is incredible and deeply satisfying.

I also relate to Dick's love for his son. My son, too, was diagnosed with cerebral palsy shortly after birth. Though not a quadriplegic, he faced challenges early on that inspire me today. With faith and grit, he's learned to face the mountain, and his doing really well.

Today, my son lives in Boston, not too far from the Boston Marathon starting line. There you will find a bronze statue of Dick pushing Rick bearing a powerful message: *"Yes You Can!"*

The Role of a Sherpa

A sherpa prioritizes their well-being to help others effectively. Just as we expect medical professionals, first responders, and soldiers to be at their best, a sherpa must be ready and acclimated.

When we take care of ourselves, we can better care for others. Acclimating means assessing the environment and understanding the needs around us. It calls for Competence, Courage, and Compassion— the qualities of a sherpa.

Unless urgent, a sherpa firsts seeks to understand before seeking to be understood. This situational awareness requires observation, information gathering, and critical thinking.

1. **Observation** – Paying attention to surroundings and then adapting.

2. **Information Gathering** – Seeking relevant information to stay informed.

3. **Critical Thinking** – Analyzing and making informed decisions to act.

Being an effective sherpa for others requires preparation in these three areas: observe, gather, and think. This is how we maximize our impact. Few embody this more than the next sherpa I want to share.

Bono – *Rock Star. Icon. Sherpa*

Bono, the legendary singer for the Irish rock band U2, serves as a modern-day sherpa, guiding others through his music and through his humanitarian advocacy.

The Edge, U2's lead guitarist and friend, states, *"Bono is the heart and soul of the band. He's the one who brings the ideas, the lyrics, the energy to the table."*

Nelson Mandela once praised Bono as a powerful advocate, calling him *"a stubborn man who would not give up"* in raising awareness for critical causes.

Bono's commitment to humanitarian work runs deep. As co-founder of The ONE Campaign and (RED), he has secured funding and influenced policies to fight poverty and HIV/AIDS in Africa. His advocacy spans human rights with Amnesty International, environmental action with Greenpeace, and palliative care with The Irish Hospice Foundation. He has supported refugees through UNHCR and provided international support for the Special Olympics.

What compels Bono to be this advocate? U2's hit song *"I Still Haven't Found What I'm Looking For"* perhaps offers a clue.

> *"I have climbed highest mountains*
> *I have run through the fields . . .*
> *I have run*
> *I have crawled*
> *I have scaled these city walls . . .*
> *But I still haven't found what I'm looking for."*

The song continues with a vision of the kingdom come, where *"all the colors will bleed into one."* It's a song of both hope and pursuit. Bono describes it as a Gospel track reflecting curiosity and renewal.[171] The author of *We Get To Carry Each Other: The Gospel According to U2* notes that it's *"not a statement of doubt, but the quintessential account of faith"* showing that God reveals things in His own time, while we have a role to play—as *"pilgrims on a journey, looking for a little elevation."*[172] And elevation requires acclimation.

Bono sees life as a journey of continuous growth, breaking free from negativity. *"It's about the quest, not the arrival,"* he says. *"That's how I find faith."*[173]

Faith Beyond Religion

Bono's dedication to compassion and community inspires others to pursue meaningful change and transform the world. In his autobiography *Surrender,* you'll find that Bono is a proponent of faith, and he values grit, which he refers to as "resolve." Yet, despite his strong faith—including being a follower of Christ[174]—he's wary of *religion,* concerned it can divide rather than unite people.[175]

His point is that religion doesn't always bring people together. It can create division. It can elicit judging, comparing, and validating (or invalidating) people. Jesus called this hypocrisy.[176] Peter, a follower of Jesus, also admonishes this.

> *"Rid yourselves of all malice and all deceit, hypocrisy, envy, and slander of every kind."*[177]

On this topic, Bono states:

> *"A religion that can so punish and degrade people is likely not being honest to God. Religion can be the biggest obstacle in your path."*[178]

With all the religions in the world, I see his point. Religion often represents a fixed mindset defined by what we think we know about God. If we are not careful, religion can introduce bias and be an obstacle to our relationships. Faith and grit, on the other hand, represent a growth mindset defined by what we don't know. They stretch us, allowing us to see beyond what we imagine.[179]

Bono's view of faith introduces the idea of companionship—and faith as a friend.

He shares, *"I view friendship as a kind of sacrament and how my traveling companion in the way of faith [has] metamorphosed from the father figure of the Old Testament to the companion and friend of the New Testament."*[180]

Faith and grit reflect a journey marked by trust with a companion and friend who walks with us, free of bias.[181] Faith means we are not alone—it's about trust.[182] Grit means not giving up—it's also about trust. This companion, who embodies these qualities, is perhaps the most important sherpa of all.

Jesus – *Shepherd. Sherpa. Savior.*

For leaders like Bono, resilience hinges on having a trusted partner to guide them up the mountain. The psalmist beautifully captures this in the 23rd Psalm:

> *The Lord is my shepherd; I shall not want.*
> *He makes me to lie down in green pastures;*
> *He leads me beside the still waters.*
> *He restores my soul;*
> *He leads me in the paths of righteousness*
> *For His name's sake.*
> *Yea, though I walk through the*
> *valley of the shadow of death,*
> *I will fear no evil;*
> *For You are with me;*
> *Your rod and Your staff, they comfort me.*
> *You prepare a table before me*
> *in the presence of my enemies;*
> *You anoint my head with oil;*
> *My cup runs over.*
> *Surely goodness and mercy shall follow me*
> *All the days of my life;*
> *And I will dwell in the house of the Lord*
> *Forever.[183]*

This timeless passage describes a Sherpa who leads us through difficult seasons and storms, assuring us that we are never alone. The Bible reveals Jesus as the fulfillment of this role, embodying the Good Shepherd who cares deeply for each of his sheep. It's not about religion; it's about a relationship.

Jesus as the Sherpa not only leads us but prepares a table for us, even in the presence of challenges. Yet, how often do we allow distractions or adversaries to take a seat at that table.[184] Even in those moments, this Sherpa seeks to fill our cup with blessings that can overflow to others. This underscores God's faithfulness and the transformative journey we're invited to take.[185]

More than just a guide, Jesus is the Savior who gave his life for us. Through his sacrifice on the cross, he opened the door to redemption and hope, offering salvation to all who believe in him.[186] This profound act of love defines his role as Savior, ensuring that no sheep is ever lost.[187]

The apostle Paul captured the essence of Christ's life in his letter to the Philippians, and I've paraphrased it into modern language. Remarkably, Paul was once the kind of man Jesus rebuked for hypocrisy but later became an advocate for unity, faith, and hope.

Here's how I imagine the apostle Paul would put it today:

> In your relationships, aim to have the same mindset as Jesus. Even though he was equal to God, he didn't cling to his position or use it for personal gain. Instead, he humbled himself, choosing to become a servant and live as a man. He stayed obedient, even to the point of death. Because of that, he earned the highest honor, and his name stands above all others. He is the Good Shepherd, guiding us through the valley and helping us face the mountain not wanting one sheep to be lost. He is there every step of the way. And, yet, he is also preparing a table for us, where one day, all the world will recognize who He is.[188]

Adopting this mindset of Jesus reminds us that it's not about religion; it's about relationships and being real. Having the mindset of Christ reshapes how we interact and connect with others. Like a shepherd, no sheep is left behind. This creates an environment where encouragement, unity, and compassion thrive. When we let go of self-interest and genuinely value others above ourselves, humility becomes a natural part of who we are.[189]

This shift strengthens relationships and builds a sense of community that stands out in a world driven by individualism. Helping people acclimate, is how we change the world.

Living with Christ's mindset means facing challenges without complaint, holding onto hope, and leading through action. It transforms us into beacons of resilience, impacting those around us. The result is profound: a life marked by integrity and a spirit that uplifts others, fostering joy and unwavering faith and grit even in difficult times.

Two guiding precepts shape this journey:

1) We are meant to walk a purposeful path, not alone.[190]

2) We are entrusted with responsibilities and called to honor others along the way.[191]

Let's unpack these precepts further:

The Journey

The precepts of God are foundational truths found in Scripture that guide us in our thoughts, actions, and decisions. These divine principles help us live in alignment with God's will, shaping a life of integrity, compassion, and wisdom. They remind us to love our neighbors, seek justice, walk humbly, and trust fully.

Embracing these precepts equips us to face life's mountains with resilience and purpose, rooted in faith and grit. These truths remind us that we are not meant to journey alone and are called to honor others while living out our purpose with courage and compassion. I want to share two of these precepts with you.

Precept 1: God Wants to Walk with Us

To understand this precept, let's explore how God acts as our Sherpa, guiding and supporting us. Here are a four scriptural statements that illustrate His involvement in our lives:

1. *"I will be with you;*
   I will never leave you nor forsake you."[192]

2. *"I will instruct you and teach you in the way you should go; I will counsel you with my loving eye on you."*[193]

3. *"So do not fear, for I am with you; do not be dismayed, for I am your God. I will strengthen you and help you; I will uphold you with my righteous right hand."*[194]

4. *"For I know the plans I have for you . . . plans to prosper you and not to harm you, plans to give you hope and a future."*[195]

These promises reveal that God is not a distant observer but an active guide who wants to be involved in every step of our journey. He offers instruction, encouragement, and unwavering support as we navigate life's challenges.

Our commitment to *face the mountain* will reveal that plan—and it will reveal His presence. The path may be steep, but with God as our Sherpa, we never need to climb alone.

Precept 2: God Entrusts Us Despite our Flaws.

What if God doesn't just want us to trust Him—what if He also wants to show that He trusts us? Yes, we're human, and we're not perfect. But perhaps God isn't looking for ability; He's looking for availability. There's a key difference.

Those who are willing and eager to follow His lead make the greatest impact. To His disciples, many who were fishermen, he simply said, "*Come, follow me.*" And they did—leaving everything behind for the sake of the call.

Consider other stories like those of Noah, Moses, Abraham, David, Daniel, and later the apostle Paul. These accounts reveal God's willingness to let ordinary people like you and me help carry out a meaningful mission and deliver a message of hope. That's God entrusting us.[196]

Here are seven things God entrusts us with, but there may be many more:

1. *The resources of the earth.*[197]
2. *Our time, talents, and treasures.*[198]
3. *Our leadership roles.*[199]
4. *Doing what's right.*[200]
5. *Teaching and instructing others.*[201]
6. *Sharing the message of grace.*[202]
7. *Helping others.*[203]

This second precept flips the perspective, suggesting that faith isn't just a one-way connection. It's not solely about us placing our faith in God as our guide; it also involves God placing trust and faith in us by giving us responsibilities on the journey. Faith, then, becomes a mutual experience, inviting us to consider the possibility that we are entrusted with a role to play in the climb.[204]

The Sherpa's Path to Leadership

These stories of Dick Hoyt, Bono, and Jesus illustrate what it takes to be a sherpa. The goal is to be a thermostat, not a thermometer—setting the temperature for others. Here are six tips to help you on the path to leadership:

Tip #1 – Let Adversity Build Character

Challenges are opportunities to grow. If the path feels too easy, we might be heading in the wrong direction. Remember the climb is going to be uphill. A sherpa needs resilience to guide others, and they must experience resistance too. Consider the impact of Walt Disney. He faced repeated setbacks on his climb to success but used adversity to strengthen him and those he led. He once said, *"a kick in the teeth may be the best thing in the world for you."*[205]

Tip #2 – Use Build-Up Thoughts

Our words shape our reality. A kind word can propel someone toward greatness, while a negative word can break their spirit. Tear-down thoughts like *"Who are you kidding? Nobody cares! You can't do that!"* limit us. Psychiatrist Dr. Daniel Amen calls these negative thoughts ANTs (Automatic Negative Thoughts). These ANTs can accumulate and hold us back.[206]

Replace these tear-down thoughts with affirmations that build resilience. As author and pastor Mark Batterson wisely said, *"Our words create worlds!"* Challenge those limiting ANTs with affirmations like *"Yes, I can!"* and *"Who says I can't?"* Use build-up thoughts to drive you forward and strengthen your journey.[207]

Tip #3 – Watch Out for Religious Bias

Leaders are called to be sherpas, guiding others on their journey. To be an effective sherpa, consider how we treat people, regardless of their background.

Growing up, I often focused on the letter of the law rather than the essence of compassion that Jesus taught.[208] Unconsciously, I started judging others based on what I thought they should be doing instead of focusing on what I ought to be doing. This mindset led to religious bias, acting more like a Pharisee than a follower of Christ.[209]

Jesus said to love God and our neighbors, emphasizing relationships over rules and religion. Religion can limit us, but faith, rooted in trust and compassion, pushes us to grow and serve others.

Tip #4 – Build Trust

Steve Jobs once said, *"Great things in business are never done by one person, they're done by a team of people."*[210] For this to happen, trust is essential. Trust means relying on your team and allowing them to rely on you. Trust multiplies impact. Jesus built trust with his disciples, inspiring lasting influence.

Charlie "Tremendous" Jones observed, *"You will be the same person in five years as you are today except for the people you meet and the books you read."*[211] Surround yourself with those who uplift you and trust them to support you. To gain trust, give trust, and be reliable. With trust, we become leaders others can depend on. For a sherpa, few things are more vital to changing the world.

Tip #5 – Let Imagination Carry You

Imagination frees us from limitations. When we harness it, we see with new eyes and recognize possibilities that once seemed out of reach. Imagine if Jesse Owens, Red McDaniel, Bono, Walt Disney, the Wright Trio or Rick Hoyt lacked the power of imagination. It's imagination—fueled by faith and grit—that propels a quadriplegic man across the Boston Marathon finish line. Imagination gives us the reason to try.

Scripture reminds us, *"Trust in the LORD with all your heart."*[212] Resilience with imagination is about the ASK: Acknowledging the need, Seeking God's wisdom, and Knocking on doors of opportunity. The ASK is when imagination meets action and faith moves us to achieve the impossible. Once our imagination is clear, it's time to go even further.

Tip #6 – Embrace a Servant Leadership Mindset

Martin Luther said, *"Faith is a living, daring confidence in God's grace, so sure and certain that a man could stake his life on it a thousand times."*[213] Grace is something leaders can reciprocate, through humility and service to others.[214] Jesus modeled servant leadership by showing compassion and understanding, even when faced with condemnation.

For instance, when religious men brought a woman accused of adultery to Jesus, demanding her punishment, he listened, then began drawing in the sand. After a moment, he looked up and said something profound: *"Let the one who has never sinned throw the first stone!"*[215] As he continued drawing, the accusers, realizing their own faults, dropped their stones and walked away. Jesus then asked the woman, *"Where are your accusers? Didn't even one of them condemn you?" "No,"* she replied. Jesus turned to her and said, *"Neither do I."*[216]

This story shows the power of leading with compassion over condemnation. Jesus, as a Sherpa, guided others with wisdom and grace, focusing on faith over religion. We should do the same. Table 3 serves as a reminder of the subtle differences.

Table 3 – Religion v. Faith

Religion	Faith
Represents what we know and think we believe	Represents what we don't yet see yet believe
Is Knowledge driven	Is Imagination fueled
Exemplifies a Fixed Mindset	Encourages a Growth Mindset (when combined with Grit)
Subconsciously used by Man to put God in a box; to define Him based on our limited thinking	Consciously used by God to get us out of our box; to refine us and expand our thinking
Characterized by rules, limits, doctrine, and order	Characterized by trust, hope, and courage
Rules focused	Relationship focused
Authoritarian leadership	Humble leadership
Trust is earned	Trust is given
Man has limits	God has no limits

True leadership is grounded in humility and centered on relationships, not rules. Therefore, prioritize compassion, humility, and service as your leadership core. As Josh McDowell said, *"Rules without relationship lead to rebellion."*[217]

Build resilience through genuine connections, avoid religious bias that divides or judges. Religion may instruct, but it is faith that truly drives us forward. Embrace a servant leadership mindset and carry that faith onto the mountain.

Action Steps

If we want to be great sherpas for others, let's remember to focus on our relationships. Being a sherpa is all about showing compassion toward others. Sherpas aid others in their ascent, but they are also making the climb themselves.

The story of Team Hoyt reminds us that we can overcome the challenges we encounter and leave a lasting impact on those around us.

What's noteworthy is that all the individuals I share about in this book had supportive figures in their lives who served as sherpas first, guiding them along the way. Remarkably, many of them, in their unique journey, eventually assumed the role of a sherpa for someone else.[218] We should do the same. Be genuinely curious about others, no matter who they are. You never know who you can help—or who might help you.

Consider these action steps to help you become a better sherpa:

1. Embrace the Role of a Sherpa

Start by revisiting the six tips for being a sherpa shared a moment ago. Each tip highlights the importance of guiding others while continuing to grow personally.

Show compassion by supporting others through their challenges, while recognizing your own path, too. Reflect on the supportive figures in your life—your Tom Hemingway's—and think about how you can play a similar role for others. Like sherpas, we grow stronger by helping others discover their path.

2. Practice Self-Care and Acclimation

Becoming a sherpa also starts with acclimation, which requires attunement. This means reading the room, observing the environment, choosing words wisely, nurturing constructive thoughts, and embodying core values.

As Jack Kornfield wisely shares, *"If your compassion does not include yourself, it remains incomplete."*[219] Prioritize emotional self-care. Just as you wouldn't climb a mountain without adequate preparation, ensure your well-being first before helping others— let your cup be full so it can overflow to help others.

3. Reflect on Your Journey and Influence

Consider the mentors and sherpas who have guided you. Think about how we can embody the qualities of a sherpa in our interactions, providing support and guidance to those who may need it. Let's become the thermostat, not just a thermometer, by setting a positive tone and influencing others constructively.

To wrap up, here are a couple of final questions to consider on this topic of being a sherpa:

1. *Who have been the sherpas and mentors in your life?* Think about the impact they made.

2. *In what ways do you serve as a sherpa for someone else?* Think about the impact YOU can make.

As you think about those who've guided you and how you can guide others, remember—we're all on this journey together. Life's not easy, but none of us need to do it alone. The goal is to help others acclimate—to be a sherpa. This is how you climb the mountain and bring others with you!

10 – Be Intentional

I once saw a billboard that said it all:

That "Love Thy Neighbor" Thing, I meant that. - God[220]

When it comes to Compassion, I think this quote pretty much reflects what it means to be intentional, don't you? Love is the greatest force for connection, empathy, and transformation. It's how hope is transferred. We just need to be intentional about it. *Being intentional* means living with hope and wanting to bring that hope to others.

The world's list of compassionate individuals who learned to be intentional despite the storms and seasons in their lives is long. I want to share a few in this chapter: a reluctant leader, a shark attack survivor, and a superhero actor who came close to taking his last breath. In the stories of their lives, we find encouragement. They exemplify Competence, Courage, and Compassion—the three essential qualities for those who *face the mountain*. However, they didn't begin with these attributes; each had to learn to adjust, acclimate, and be intentional in the midst of challenges.

Fred Rogers – *Bullied Compassionate Survivor*

Fred Rogers had a challenging childhood, marked by struggles with weight and frequent illness. He was often bullied at school. In high school, he overcame his extreme shyness and began intentionally building friendships. Before long, he ran for president of the school council and became the editor in chief of the school yearbook.

After college, which included time at a theological seminary, Rogers found his way into public television. He dedicated his life to creating a children's show that helped both young and old see the beauty in each day.

His show, *Mister Rogers' Neighborhood,* aired for thirty-one seasons. Compassionate might as well have been his middle name— it's what being a good neighbor is all about.

I heard my favorite story of Mr. Rogers firsthand from my in-laws. They were traveling through western Pennsylvania in the early '90s when their car broke down on the highway. A passing motorist in a blue Chevrolet Impala pulled over to help change their tire. To their surprise, it was none other than Fred Rogers and his wife, Joanne.

Mister Rogers himself helped my father-in-law fix a flat. How cool is that!

Here's a fitting quote from Fred Rogers:

> *"All of us, at some time or other, need help. Whether we're giving or receiving help, each of us has something valuable to bring to this world. That's one of the things that connects us as neighbors—in our own way, each one of us is a giver and a receiver."*[221]

Bethany Hamilton – *Shark Attack Survivor*

Born with her family's passion for the water, young Bethany Hamilton loved surfing and competing. She couldn't get enough of it. While out on a routine practice ride off the North Shore of Kauai, a fourteen-foot tiger shark snuck up on her and mauled her, resulting in the loss of her left arm. Her family and friends were devastated. But somehow, Bethany rose above the tragedy; her aspiration to surf again only grew stronger, and she became intentional, fighting through the pain with an attitude that helped her acclimate and inspire others.

Bethany shared her outlook. *"I've learned life is a lot like surfing. When you get caught in the impact zone, you need to get right back up, because you never know what's over the next wave."* Her use of the phrase *impact zone* is what I mean when I say potential zone. Bethany adds, *"If you have faith, anything is possible, anything at all."*[222]

Being intentional in our pursuits teaches us to be intentional in helping others with theirs. One of my favorite scenes illustrating this intentionality is from the film *Soul Surfer*, which portrays her life. Despite a strong desire to surf again, Bethany is nearing a breaking point. All she sees are her limitations. In frustration, she cries out to her father, Tom Hamilton, played by actor Dennis Quaid, *"I'm done . . . I can't even paddle out to the line past the big waves. I don't understand what happened to . . . 'I can do all things.'"* She continues. *"Why? Why did this happen? Why did I have to lose everything?"*[223]

In that emotional moment, Bethany is overwhelmed by her limitations. She struggles with her inability to surf as she used to.

Her dad responds with compassion, reminding her that she hasn't lost everything. He points out that she's still alive and has the support of her family. He starts to shift her focus from what she has lost to what she still has. Despite his reassurance, Bethany remains uncertain about her future and seeks further guidance. Tom acknowledges that he doesn't have all the answers but encourages her to be patient and listen for what comes next, assuring her that in time, clarity will come.

Fast-forward a few scenes later, and we see Bethany with a new resolve. She has now locked in on her values and realizes that life isn't about what she gets; it's about what she gets to give.

She realizes her passion is still there—it's a compassion for people. *"Surfing isn't the most important thing in life. Love is. I've had the chance to embrace more people with one arm than I ever could with two."* She encourages us further, *"Compassion can drive us to do amazing things and give us perspective."*[224]

Jeremy Renner – *Snowcat Survivor*

Bethany Hamilton's story pairs nicely with a similar story that took the world by surprise. On January 1, 2023, actor Jeremy Renner, best known for his iconic role as Hawkeye in *"The Avengers"* and his role as Mike McLusky in *"Mayor of Kingstown,"* was spending time with his family during the New Year's break at his winter home in Nevada. Over a three-day period, approximately twelve feet of snow blanketed their property. Wanting to seize on the opportunity to enjoy the beautiful outdoors to start the new year, Renner fired up his snowcat (also known as a snow groomer) early in the morning to clear out the neighborhood driveway and road.

As he was cleaning out the lot, he sensed a potential problem when his snowcat began slipping on the ice. He jumped out while it was still running, simply to alert his nephew to move his truck that was potentially on a path of being sideswiped. Just as he was jumping back in the snowcat to man the controls, his foot caught one of the moving tracks, and he was catapulted off the rig and onto the icy asphalt.

Before he knew it, the fourteen-hundred-pound snowcat ran over his body, crushing thirty-eight bones, puncturing his lung, and detaching his eye from its socket. His nephew scrambled up the icy hill to find him barely alive and called out for help.

Within an hour, Renner was airlifted to the hospital and put on life support for over three days. He underwent multiple surgeries. Today, despite all his injuries, surgeries, and rehab, Renner is back on the job, with broken bones repaired or replaced with titanium and a reconstructed face that looks just like it did before.

Reflecting on the accident with his friend Jimmy Fallon on *The Tonight Show* in May 2024, Renner shared a profound perspective: *"I won't have a bad day for the rest of my life. It's impossible."*[225]

That's the message I want to remember for my life, too, when I reflect on The Hook, where I could have lost it all. It provides perspective.

Reflecting on that whole ordeal, Fallon admitted his fear when he heard the news. *"I thought we lost you."*

"For a second, we did," Renner replied with emotion. *"But I got some duct tape and stuck it all back together. We're good."*[226]

The smile that Fallon and Renner exchange is genuine. For Fallon, it was a relief to know that someone he cared for so much was given a second chance.

After the injury, Renner was told he may never walk normally again. A complete recovery looked impossible, but today, he is back to work. His life may never be the same, but he knows that with resilience, he can *face the mountain.*

In an interview with the *CBS Mornings* crew, Renner shared that the impact of others in his life helped drive him hard in his rehab, starting with his daughter. *"She was afraid,"* admitted Renner. *"But everything I did was to show her that I was getting better. She was my driving force."* Renner adds, *"I relieved myself of whatever I had to go through. And the more I healed, [the more] I'd heal my mother, my poor nephew, who had to hold my arms [and] watch me [almost] die on the ice. The better I get, the better they get. They were my fuel."*[227]

On *The Tonight Show*, he shared with Fallon that his greatest lesson from the accident was simple: *"step by step."* When it comes to being intentional, there may be nothing more profound. This may be the same lesson that Fred Rogers, Bethany Hamilton, or any intentional sherpa might share with you, too.

This brings me back to a comment Renner shared with Fallon about being intentional. *"If we get too stressed or if things get too difficult or if it's insurmountable odds or whatever it might be, just put one foot down and then put another foot down and move towards it."* [228]

Step by step.[229]

What Does It Mean to Be Intentional?

Hope is not merely a fleeting emotion but a powerful force that can uplift and transform us and those around us. When we embrace this intentionality, we become bearers of hope—something the world desperately needs.

Here are five steps to be intentional with hope:

Step 1 – Practice Empathy

Start by trying to understand the feelings and experiences of those around you. Empathy is the foundation of intentional hope. It allows us to connect with others on a deeper level. When we see the world through their eyes, we can offer hope that truly resonates.

Hope can be a beacon of light in a world filled with uncertainty and challenges—a gift to ourselves and those around us. However, we must tread carefully. Charles Spurgeon once said, *"The greatest enemy to human souls is the self-righteous spirit."*[230] If we are not careful, our desire to be intentional can turn into self-righteousness. That's why empathy is crucial. It keeps us grounded and prevents us from thinking too highly of ourselves.

Step 2 – Make Today Count

Our words and deeds carry power. When used with care and intention, they can encourage and inspire. They shape the world around us, fostering hope not just for ourselves but for others. This is how we shift from being thermometers to thermostats. From reacting to the world around us, to setting the tone for others.

To help create meaningful impact, here's a ten-point guide inspired by the wisdom of Dr. William Arthur Ward.[231]

1) *Today we can be GRATEFUL*

By appreciating life, friends, opportunities, and God's blessings. Gratitude can shift our focus from what's wrong to what's right.

2) Today we can be CHEERFUL

By offering a smile, sharing a kind word, or reflecting a positive attitude with those we meet. Good cheer has the power to change the room.

3) Today we can be OPTIMISTIC

By expecting good things to happen to and through us. Hope opens the door to new possibilities. By choosing optimism, we invite creativity, connection, and growth.

4) Today we can be in PRAYER

By taking a moment to share our desires for ourselves and others we recharge spiritually and refresh mentally. Prayer helps us to let go of worries and find peace.

5) Today we can be UNSELFISH

By applying the Golden Rule in our thoughts, words, and actions, we do for others what we would want done for ourselves. Being unselfish helps change the world.

6) Today we can look for the BEST in others

By seeing the value in those around us, believing in their potential, and celebrating their strengths and gifts, we inspire ourselves to see those qualities within. When we focus on what's right and catch the good in others, it inspire us to see it in ourselves as well.

7) Today we can spread JOY

By sharing a thoughtful gesture, kind act, word of encouragement, or amusing story, we bring delight to others. These moments—a smile, wave, or shared laughter—create a ripple effect that multiplies joy.

8) *Today we can be FORGIVING*

By letting go of resentment, grudges, and bitterness, and embracing understanding and compassion—forgiveness frees us from negative emotions. It brings us peace.

9) *Today we can be GENEROUS*

By offering our time, resources, or kindness to others, generosity becomes an open-hearted choice that positively impacts others.

10) *Today we can be PRESENT*

By engaging fully with the moment, recognizing "right now" is a gift, we embrace the present and life's blessings.

Small acts of kindness—like a smile, a helping hand, or a thoughtful gesture—spread hope in powerful ways. These ten simple actions, which any of us can do *today*, have the potential to make a significant impact on the lives of others. Imagine the compound impact over time. This is how we can live intentionally.

Step 3 – Lead by Example

Whether we realize it or not, people around us observe our actions, attitudes, and behaviors. This means we influence others—either positively or negatively. *So why not choose to lead with hope?*

Every choice we make, every challenge we face, and how we respond to adversity serves as a model for others to follow. Our influence ripples out far beyond what we might imagine.

The key is to model the behavior we want to see in others. By maintaining a positive outlook and persevering through challenges, we inspire those around us. Our actions become a guiding light for those who struggle. This leads us back to empathy, which may be the best way to lead by example.

In a world hungry for hope, being intentional in our actions can be a life-changing gift. When we practice empathy, choose positive language, perform acts of kindness, and lead by example, we help create a more hopeful and compassionate world.

Step 4 – Recognize You Are in the Hope Business

Aristotle describes hope as a "waking dream."[232] Jonas Salk said, *"Hope lies in dreams, in imagination, and in the courage of those who dare to make dreams into reality."*[233]

Hope isn't just a wish you wait for—it's something you pursue. Hope activates faith and grit, as it reflects trust, confidence, and resilience. Can you see hope's connection with faith and grit? Hope operates at every level of belief.[234]

To examine your hopes for each level, consider these five questions:

1. Do you have hope in the **infrastructure** around you?
2. Do you have hope in the **systems** you use?
3. Do you have hope in the **people** around you?
4. Do you have hope in your **strengths** and **abilities**?
5. Do you have hope in a **higher power**?

Our answers reveal our active state of resilience and what others see from us. They reveal our hope quotient (HQ). But what about those around us? Understanding their hopes enables us to serve them with more intention.

Here are four key actions we can take to unlock this step:

A. Understand the Mission

Our life's mission is to be in the hope business, twenty-four seven. Imagine the impact at home, at work, and in the community. The services we offer, the products we build, and the value we add are more meaningful when they fulfill a hope. People are drawn to what fulfills their hopes—that's the real solution they seek. That's what they want to buy.

But lasting hope doesn't come from things; it comes from the love and support of others. Let's be beacons of hope, shining like lights on a hill for those facing the mountain.

B. Identify the Vision

George Washington Carver once said, *"Where there is no vision, there is no hope."*[235] Eleanor Roosevelt echoed this sentiment: *"If you lose faith, you lose all.*"[236] Both suggest that vision and faith are essential for overcoming challenges and achieving success.

Building resilience starts by helping others recognize hope. Without hope, the imagination can drift into dark places, fueling fears, worries, and doubts. But with hope, the imagination reveals where faith and grit can lead. Hope is the starting point of vision.

It's important to remember that what we envision is often what we achieve. When hope fades, faith feels hollow. Without the ability to see new possibilities, it's hard to have grit. Faith and grit tied to vision are what get us out of bed each day, with hope serving as the catalyst.

The goal here is simple: help others be resilient by giving them a vision of what can be.

C. *Help Others Find Purpose*

One scripture serves as a powerful reminder about our future:

"For I know the plans I have for you . . . plans to prosper you and not to harm you, plans to give you hope and a future."[237]

This passage reminds us that no matter how things seem, better opportunities lie ahead. Our purpose isn't defined by our past; it's defined by our potential.

What if we could help people find their purpose, get clear on their plan, and offer them hope?

We can start by helping them reflect on their strengths, passions, and values, then guide them to identify actionable steps toward their future. If appropriate, share that they are not alone, that's there is a God who cares about them.

For millions, hope has a name: God. Ninety percent of Americans believe in a higher power; 56% percent profess faith in God as described in the Bible.[238] For them, hope reflects God's attributes. This can be seen in the names *Emmanuel* meaning "God Is with Us," and *Jesus,* from the Hebrew word *Yeshua,* meaning "to rescue or to deliver."[239]

But let's help people, regardless of their belief system. We may not share the same theology, but we share the same physiology. Let's help others reflect on their strengths. encourage them to consider their passions and values, and guide them to take one actionable step toward their future. Let's give them hope! And, if it helps, let's let them know where we find our source of hope.

If you know someone struggling, remind them that holding on to past regrets—or even past successes—limits potential. It keeps us stuck. The past isn't meant to overshadow the future. By focusing on the present and the potential ahead, we discover our purpose. With purpose, the best is yet to come, but we still need our imagination to be resilient.

D. *Leverage Imagination*

To execute our mission, vision and purpose, we need to paint a plan. This is where imagination comes into play. Knowing what we want requires imaginative thinking to help us see the plan and identify an approach.

The Greek philosopher Plato referred to imagination as the ability to reason.[240] The original Hebrew and Greek texts of the Bible use three ancient words associated with this idea: *chashabh*, *hagah*, and *meletao*.

- *Chashabh* (Hebrew) means *"to think, plan, devise, esteem, calculate, invent."*[241] In the New American Standard version of the Bible, this verb is linked to one hundred and twenty-two verses in the Old Testament.[242]

- *Hagah* (Hebrew) and *Meletao* (Greek) both mean *"to meditate."*[243] *Hagah* is linked multiple times in the Old Testament[244], whereas *Meletao* is used in the New Testament.[245]

As a fun challenge, I encourage you to explore the scriptures and look for verb phrases like *"think," "think about," "think of," "meditate," "meditate on," "reason,"* or *"look at,"* and try substituting each with the word *"imagine."* Similarly, when you encounter the noun phrase *"thoughts,"* replace it with the word *"imagination."*

To help you with this exercise, I have identified a handful of passages in Table 4 showing you this scripture treatment. It highlights how the use of the word "imagine" brings new insights into how we should live.

It encourages us at all Five Levels of Belief as discussed in Chapter 4. When we root our hope in our vision, our imagination will reveal what can be. Take a minute to reflect on these thoughts, and see how they tie to hope.

Table 4 – A Fresh Look at Imagination in the Bible

Verse	Level
Do not worry about your life, what you will eat or what you will drink. . . . *IMAGINE* the birds of the air; for they neither sow nor reap nor gather into barns; yet your heavenly Father feeds them. Are you not of more value than they?[246]	1
Give attention to reading, to exhortation, to doctrine . . . *IMAGINE* these things; give yourself entirely to them, that your progress may be evident to all. Take heed to yourself and to the doctrine. Continue in them, for in doing this you will save both yourself and those near you.[247]	2
Let us *IMAGINE* ways to motivate one another to acts of love and good works. [248]	3
For as he *IMAGINES* in his heart, so is he.[249]	4
Those who are dominated by the sinful nature *IMAGINE* sinful things, but those who are controlled by the Holy Spirit *IMAGINE* things that please the Spirit.[250]	4
Fix your *IMAGINATION* on what is true, and honorable, and right, and pure, and lovely, and admirable. *IMAGINE* things that are excellent and worthy of praise. [251]	4
IMAGINE the Lord and his strength; seek his face always. Remember the wonders he has done, his miracles. [252]	5
His power at work in us can do far more than we dare ask or *IMAGINE*. [253]	5
IMAGINE the things of heaven, not the things of earth.[254]	5
Look! I am creating new heavens and a new earth, and no one will even *IMAGINE* the old ones anymore.[255]	5

It's a fresh new way to look at scripture, isn't it?

Action Steps

This chapter focused on being intentional for those facing the mountain. The stories we explored, including those of Fred Rogers, Bethany Hamilton, and Jeremy Renner. Being intentional involves understanding our mission, identifying our vision, finding our purpose, and cultivating hope. It's about being a good neighbor and helping others on the journey.

Here are the steps to put into play:

1. Practice Empathy

Understand and share the feelings of others. This means listening carefully and responding with compassion, acknowledging their struggles and offering support.

2. Make Each Day Count

Be purposeful in your actions and decisions. Each day presents an opportunity to make a positive impact, no matter how small. Focus on what you can do today to contribute to your mission and vision.

3. Lead by Example

Demonstrate the behaviors and attitudes you wish to see in others. Your actions should align with your values and purpose, serving as a model for those around you.

4. Be in the Hope Business

Acknowledge the power you have to inspire and uplift others. Your words and actions can instill hope and encourage others to find their own purpose and path. By being a source of hope, you not only uplift others but also strengthen your own sense of purpose. Remember, your mission gains meaning as you help others discover theirs. Let hope guide both your actions and your journey forward.

Take a moment to reflect on these steps. *What one action can you take to increase your compassion?*

11 — CULTIVATE CARE

"If you can't feed a hundred people,
then feed just one."
–Mother Teresa

merican football fans sat in silence for Damar Hamlin as he lay motionless on the turf while medical staff worked feverishly to revive him. Players from both teams circled together. They were in shock. The game itself quickly became an afterthought. It was all about Damar—a human life whose heart had stopped. Things looked grim.

Soon, people started praying at the stadium, in front of their TVs, and at their computers. Prayer chains began circulating in emails, Facebook threads, and X posts. My wife, who is not even a football fan, got a ding on her phone to pray. For a brief period of time, prayer brought part of the world together. We held on to hope.

The following day, we woke up in wonder. *"Did he make it?"* The answer was YES! Our hope was still alive. Today, Damar Hamlin is a walking miracle despite suffering a cardiac arrest after a routine tackle in a football game.

Resilience without hope is like an empty cup; it can only take us so far without water. Hope represents the water that quenches our thirst, and one way to taste that water is through prayer.

In a world that needs hope, why wouldn't we want to unite in prayer? Prayer allows us to cultivate care. This should be our first line of support no matter what the circumstance.

What Is Prayer?

Prayer is expressing our heart's *desires* to God. When done collectively, it becomes corporate prayer, which is the shared expression of those desires with others. The word *desire* originates from the Latin word *desiderare*, meaning a longing or strong wish for something.[256]

We all experience desire, and have a wish for something. It's a natural human condition. Desire reflects what we hope for or aspire to be. Napoleon Hill emphasizes its importance: *"The starting point of all achievement is desire."* He urges us to *"keep this constantly in mind."*[257]

That sounds a lot like prayer, doesn't it?

Saint Augustine affirms, *"The desire is thy prayers."*[258]

C. S. Lewis echoes this sentiment, calling prayer *"a form of request."*[259] He offers a personal insight into his own prayer life:

> *"I pray because I can't help myself.*
> *I pray because I'm helpless.*
> *I pray because the need flows out of me all the time,*
> *waking and sleeping.*
> *It doesn't change God. It changes me."*[260]

Desire. Prayer. Change. That's what gets us up the hill. And the best way to focus the mind on the climb is through prayer.

But to whom do we direct our prayers?

The Bible says to *"let all who are faithful offer prayer to you,"* referring to God, the Creator of the universe.[261] King David embodied this sentiment during his many trials, directing his prayers to God as he faced his own mountains. Many of the Psalms stand as letters of those prayers; they echo our resilience through God's strength.[262]

At its core, prayer is mental focus on what we hope for, over what we fear. This ties to what Brian Tracy states regarding success. *"The key to success is to focus our conscious mind on things we desire not things we fear."*[263]

The most profound desire we can express is gratitude, not just hope. German philosopher Meister Eckhart encapsulates this beautifully:

> *"If the only prayer you ever say in your entire life is thank you, it will be enough."*[264]

The transformative power of gratitude in our prayer life, can be a difference maker.

Simple Guidelines for Prayer

Prayer is one of the most intentional mental actions we can take. It doesn't require religion; it just requires faith and grit.

As mentioned earlier, Jesus encourages us to ask, seek, and knock—three actions that encompass the essence of prayer.[265]

- If you need something, ask.

- If you feel worried, seek hope.

- If you want opportunities, knock.

These three actions reflect a posture of prayer that can be seen in the four key parts of the Lord's Prayer, which guide us in how we approach God:

1) Acknowledge God

2) Seek Provision

3) Express Hope

4) Be Open and Sincere

Part 1 – Acknowledge God

The first part of the Lord's Prayer teaches us to *praise* God before making requests, establishing trust across all Five Levels of Belief. Meaning it's God who provides for our physical, emotional, mental and spiritual needs.

> *Our Father in heaven,*
> *Hallowed be Your name.*
> *Your kingdom come.*
> *Your will be done*
> *On earth as it is in heaven.*[266]

Part 2 – Seek Provision

This focuses on *asking* for our needs and forgiving others.

> *Give us this day our daily bread.*
> *And forgive us our debts,*
> *As we forgive our debtors.*[267]

Part 3 - Express Hope

Here, we express our hopes and ask for protection as we step out of our comfort zone and face that mountain.

> *And do not lead us into temptation.*
> *But deliver us from the evil one.*

Part 4 - Be Open and Sincere

Prayer itself represents *knocking*—being open and sincere with God and welcoming opportunities where we can make a difference. We pray not to force God to act, we pray so that we can *face the mountain* with His presence.

Like the opening of the Lord's Prayer, it closes with the acknowledgement of His dominion.

> *For Yours is the kingdom and the power and the glory forever. Amen.*[268]

The Benefits of Prayer

Consider the benefits of prayer as it relates to care. Expressing our desires can be crucial for our mental health; otherwise, desires bottled up become emotions that boil over. Prayer provides a way to release these emotions before fear and worry lead to frustration or hostility. Prayer is a way to lean on hope and reduce fear.

Prayer is also a multiplier—it's a way to express hope for others. It can serve this purpose in four ways:

1. **Intercession**

   When we pray for others, we intercede on their behalf. By lifting up their needs, concerns, and desires, we express our hope for positive outcomes in their lives. This act of intercession can have a ripple effect, influencing the lives of those we pray for and potentially bringing about positive changes. It activates the Reticular Activating System (RAS), a component of the brain used to seek and find.[269]

2. **Unity and Support**

   In corporate prayer, a group of people come together to pray for a common cause of individuals in need. This act creates a sense of unity and support. Knowing that others pray for them can comfort and encourage those facing challenges or difficult situations. This collective expression of hope strengthens bonds within communities and fosters a sense of solidarity. This is what we saw with Damar Hamlin.

3. **Spiritual Impact**

    Prayer invites divine intervention, requesting God's participation. It reflects a trust that God will somehow provide despite our challenges. The word's prayers for Damar Hamlin and Jeremy Renner exemplified this. Both were on their deathbed, but through collective faith and grit—through prayer and care—that fatal script was rewritten. Because of that, they are now both walking miracles.

4. **Positive Momentum**

    Prayer generates positive momentum. When we sincerely pray for the well-being and success of others, we send out good intentions. It's what people need to hear. This creates an atmosphere of encouragement that uplifts people's spirits and helps them see hopeful outcomes. Hope is a great motivator.

The bottom line is that prayer is a multiplier, reflecting our care for others. It underscores our needs and hopes, fosters connection, and embodies the strength of our collective faith and grit. Prayer also connects us to God, inviting His participation. Yet, the true power of prayer isn't always in the asking; it's in the waiting and listening. That's when our brains are rewired.

Your Brain on Prayer

A study by researchers at the University of Pennsylvania shows that prayer does the body good—or, in this case, the brain. They discovered that praying increases our dopamine levels.[270]

Dopamine is a chemical messenger that creates a feeling of satisfaction and is how the brain rewards progress. It's a powerful neurotransmitter. The natural increase of dopamine that prayer offers creates a sense of hope and assurance.

As a test to show you what I mean, I want you to think about something you want or hope for—something you desire. *Do you have it in mind?* The mere thought of something you hope for triggers a small drip of dopamine that regulates mood and motivation. It supports learning, memory, focus, movement. Balanced dopamine is key to mental well-being and the pursuit of rewarding experiences. When we experience hope, it fuels us with a healthy dose of dopamine, benefiting both mind and body.

I'll never forget the day that my mentor, John Maxwell, personally prayed for me after learning about a serious health challenge I was walking through. It's a prayer that changed my life.

Less than a half year earlier, I lost partial vision in my left eye. It knocked me for a loop. A few days later, I received my diagnosis: optic neuritis in my left eye. But that wasn't the devastating news; it was that the optic neuritis might be a sign of Multiple Sclerosis (MS). I was in disbelief and, for a brief period of time, inconsolable.

It only grew worse when I researched it. My imagination took me down some dark alleyways of the challenges I might face. An MRI a few days later confirmed the diagnosis. I had MS. For two weeks, I began to slowly resign to a worst-case scenario that it might eventually lead to immobility. The more research I did on the web, the more paralyzing it became.

But then I began hearing stories of others with MS who found a way to press on. It renewed in me a flame of hope. I realized that there are things I could do to treat and manage it. The MS didn't need to own me. I could somehow own it.

However, the trigger that put me in the "right frame of mind" was that prayer months later from John Maxwell. He caught me in a hotel hallway after somehow finding out the news. During our discussion I shared more of my story, and he asked if he could pray for me. Of course, I said yes.

He prayed for my health—and my resilience. He asked God to direct my steps and the steps of my family walking with me. He shared a vision that this unexpected challenge wouldn't limit me from being who I was called to be but might be used instead to encourage and uplift others. This amazing prayer bolstered my spirits.

Hours later, as I thought about that hallway encounter, I realized that his prayer wasn't just meant for me—it was meant for anyone facing the mountain. Each step is an important step in our climb. With each step, we can affect change, show compassion, and equip others. We can turn our challenges into ways to inspire others, because we all have mountains to face.

I look back on that day and see that prayer restored my mental vision for my life. It brought back Tom Hemingway's words that every day is a gift. *"Now what am I going to do with it?"* I clearly see it now. It isn't over if we fall; it's only over when we choose to quit.

◆　◆　◆

For more about my MS story and the impact of John Maxwell's prayer, I encourage you to read chapter 9 of my book *IMAGINE*.

Also, be sure to check out the Climber's Prayer in the appendix of this book. Prayer helps us face our daily mountains, reminding us to trust in something greater than ourselves. It's a tool of resilience, but we still need to put in the effort. This brings me to one of my favorite quotes from the philosopher, Saint Augustine. [271]

"Pray as Though Everything Depends on God . . ."

Prayer isn't just a wish-a-thon event like blowing out candles on a birthday cake or tossing a coin in a fountain, hoping for good luck. Prayer represents honest, two-way communication—sharing our needs and wants, and believing that God is listening. In prayer, we should share our needs, seek to understand what God wants, and strive to be thankful for whatever will come.

The apostle Paul shares this tip:

> *"Don't worry about anything; instead, pray about everything. Tell God what you need, and thank him for all he has done. Then you will experience God's peace, which exceeds anything we can understand."*[272]

The steps are clear: identify what worries or concerns you, think through what requests you have, and then package them up in prayer, thanking God in advance for however He will answer them.

If we look at the Psalms in the Old Testament, we see this treatment in these written prayers. They often start with a worry, concern, or plea and end with a healthy view of God's blessings.

The apostle Paul further encourages us with these words:

> *"Finally, brothers and sisters, whatever is true, whatever is noble, whatever is right, whatever is pure, whatever is lovely, whatever is admirable—if anything is excellent or praiseworthy—think about such things.*

. . . And the God of peace will be with you."[273]

Prayer can transform anxiety or worry into hope and healing. Look to see hope realized. Just as football fans did for Damar Hamlin, share your hope by praying with and for others. When prayer is rooted in care, it unites people in their common desires.

Prayer is meant to be rooted in hope, not doubt.

> *"When you pray, you must believe and not doubt."*[274]
> *"God is able to do far more than we could ever ask for or imagine."*[275]

The Bible gives us the reason for this hope:

> *"For I know the plans I have for you, declares the Lord, plans to prosper you and not to harm you, plans to give you hope and a future."*[276]

When we pray, let's do so with unwavering hope and confidence, trusting that our deepest desires and needs are understood beyond what we can imagine. Believe that every prayer, grounded in faith and hope, aligns with a greater purpose designed to guide us toward a future filled with meaning.

". . . Work as Though Everything Depends on You!"

Faith expressed through prayer requires action—that's the grit component. When we pray earnestly, we're presenting our desires to God while also priming our brain to seek and help bring those answers into being. Prayer isn't just a request for divine intervention; it's a two-party commitment. Prayers backed by action demonstrate our resilience and rekindle hope in others.

God responds to the ask, sees what we seek, and hears the knock. But we also have a responsibility to keep seeking and knocking. The Sherpa doesn't climb the mountain for us. We need to put skin in the game, too.

Once we make our requests known, it's time to take action while we continue to pray. *What paths will we explore? On which doors will we knock?*

A person of prayer is a person of hope. But hope needs action. Otherwise, it's just a wish. Hope is a collaborative sport; we all need to do our part. Hope requires action to win the battle.

Top Ten Productivity Tips You've Heard Before

One of my mentors, Ed DeCosta, who recently passed, once shared a great strategy for taking action that I want to pass on to you:[277]

1. Rise Early! (*and pray!*)
2. Review/tweak the plan for the day.
3. Do important things first.
4. No multitasking.
5. Avoid interruptions.
6. Work your plan.
7. Take mini breaks every ~90 minutes.
8. Eat small, frequent meals.
9. Get your heart rate up by moving.
10. End the day by planning for tomorrow.

Repeat ☺

I love Ed's list. Even though he is gone, his legacy lives on. Ed was a go-getter, and he genuinely cared for people. That's a great combination. The most productive people on the planet are those who live with hope.

Praying Solitaire – *My Father's Routine*

Few things are more encouraging and caring than the thoughtful prayers of others. After my dad passed in 2007, we found a multipage list of handwritten names and needs, each marked with dates. It was his prayer ledger.

On the list were his pencil marks for each request. For many of the needs, there were notes of how prayers were being answered. It blew us away.

All those times we thought he had been playing Solitaire mindlessly on his computer in his office was a ruse. He was in prayer, marking that sheet, spending an hour or more lifting each request to God. I picture how each card on Solitaire was mentally marked by a name from that list and then prayed over. The game was only won when he prayed over every name. He would then go upstairs and spend time with Mom.

Looking back, I can see evidence that my dad's prayer life probably saved me a time or two. There was that time in college, my first year when I almost went off the rails, but he and others who he called on for prayer support, well—they prayed for a hedge of protection to surround me and averted disaster. There were other moments like this, too. He quietly prayed for the different needs of all my children and my wife. His handwritten prayer list was like a master's journal marking prayer requests and prayers answered.

After my father passed away, I felt a noticeable void in the steady support I had always relied on. His earnest prayers for me and our family had been a source of strength and reassurance. In his absence, I found myself searching for others who could fill the role he once held. Knowing that someone interceded for me brought comfort and nourished my hope during challenging times.

I want the kind of prayer life that my dad had, but maybe without the Solitaire. However, what I learned from his Solitaire praying practice is that we can habit-stack praying with something else. Maybe it's praying while taking a walk or when cutting the grass or brushing our teeth.

What prayers can we ask the God of the universe—not just for ourselves, but for others? Remember the power of asking. Often, our desires go unanswered because we do not ask. *What do you need? What do others need? What do you hope for?*

Let's take time to make our requests known. Like my dad, what if we captured the various ways our prayers are answered. Let that list encourage us—and others! And if someone can pray specifically for you in an hour of need, then go ahead and let them.

Action Steps

In matters of hope, never underestimate the value of prayer. The pathway is clear: Imagination drives Faith. Faith promotes Prayer. Prayer increases Dopamine. Dopamine spurs Hope. And Hope fuels Grit. It goes full circle.

This chapter has focused on the power of care as an essential habit for compassion. Marian Wright Edelman once said, "*You really can change the world if you care enough.*"[278]

Prayer is a core tool for care, allowing us to bring our hearts before God. It's about expressing the desires we hold for ourselves and those we care about. This act of reaching out to God activates resilience, engaging our minds with positive intent as we await for answers, but it also prompts us to seek solutions and fulfill needs.

Here are four action steps to cultivate care through prayer:

1. *Acknowledge*

Recognize and express gratitude for the blessings in your life. Acknowledging the good fosters a positive mindset and appreciation for what you have.

2. *Share Your Need*

Openly express your needs and concerns. This step is about being honest with yourself, with others, and with God, allowing you to confront and address challenges.

3. *Express Your Hope*

Convey your hopes and aspirations. Articulating these desires helps clarify your goals and motivates you to work toward them.

4. *Be Open and Sincere*

Approach prayer with an open heart, being sincere in your words and intentions. This authenticity deepens your connection and makes the practice more meaningful.

Let our prayers be the foundation of a compassionate heart, bringing hope to ourselves and those around us.

Studies show that prayer, when tied to belief, can improve how we respond to medical treatment. People who lean on their faith and pray, *"have better mental health and adapt more quickly"* to health challenges.[279]

Take a moment to reflect on this lesson. What is one small step you can take to make prayer a habit? Consider how prayer allows you to be a beacon of hope for others who also *face the mountain*. Finally, think about how prayer can change the world.

12 – DO IT ANYWAY

This book has explored the importance of Competence, Courage, and Compassion as we *face the mountain*. It's how we measure success. I want to share one more thing that brings all of this together; I think it's a game changer.

Every Day Is Practice

There's a great phrase used in sports that's more than a cliché.

*"Practice like you'll play because
you'll play like you practiced."*[280]

The first time I heard this was when I played competitive travel soccer. My coach, Jack Bergen, whom we called Coach B, believed that to win on Sunday, we needed to win at practice beforehand. If he saw you holding back, he'd pull you to the side and gently ask you what the point of practice was. Coach B was a 3C leader—especially on Compassion.

I used to think that practice was a time to connect with teammates, knock the ball around a bit, and talk about the upcoming game. But Coach B taught us that it was more than that. Practice was a proving ground to show we were ready. It's where we executed the strategy, not just talked about it. How we practiced was how we played on game day. Our team collected our fair share of hardware over the next few seasons to prove it.

Tom Hemingway was trained to lead as a Marine and was called to be a leader of leaders. Likewise, Coach B, a former Army Ranger and graduate of the U.S. Military Academy at West Point, was also called to lead others. His military training taught him the importance of practice, a principle he brought to the soccer field. He focused on training and equipping others to be strategic through consistent practice. Practice builds confidence; every day is an opportunity to build that confidence, which ultimately stems from competence.

For our soccer team, I remember practice had an element of competition tied to a learning objective. It's also where he put in the work. And we did, too. Our confidence grew before game day, so that when Sundays finally came, those days were easy. We stepped onto the field 100 percent ready. Our best games were won long before Sunday. Mentors are those who will ready their teams before the battle.

In the military, a soldier's effectiveness depends on training. Practice doesn't make perfect, but perfect practice prepares one better for the task. That's the essence of the *Face the Mountain* mindset. Those who prepare turn the tide; they become Competent, Courageous, and Compassionate.

Drawing from my mentors, starting with Coach B, I've distilled seven rules for resilience that reinforce the 3Cs of Resilience. These Seven Rules aren't for the faint of heart—they're for those ready to *face the mountain*, knowing that every day is a dress rehearsal for success.

Seven Daily Rules to Practice Resilience

Rule #1 - Face the Doubt

Let's be honest. Doubt can take us out of the game before it even starts. I once saw a meme that said, *"Doubt will kill more dreams than failure ever will."*[281] I think this is true. On game day, Coach B ensured that doubt never joined us on the bus. He did this by nipping it in the bud at practice, teaching us to recognize and identify it. That's because he cared for us.

When imagination is tied to doubt or fear, it often paints a gloomy outcome.[282] But how does that serve us?

Each one of us experiences doubt. Like cancer, doubt can grow and build. It can throw us off in our pursuit of a dream. What's required is to face the doubt head-on with faith and grit. This is what resilience is all about.

Jesus makes a profound statement in the gospels.

> *"Have faith in God. . . . Truly I tell you, if anyone says to this mountain, 'Go, throw yourself into the sea,' and does not doubt in their heart but believes that what they say will happen, it will be done."*[283]

He then emphasizes a critical point.

> *"I tell you, whatever you ask for in prayer, believe that you have received it, and it will be yours."*[284]

Later, James reemphasizes this critical point in one of his letters.

> *"When you ask, you must believe and not doubt, because the one who doubts is like a wave of the sea, blown and tossed by the wind."*[285]

James then shares that doubt makes us *"double-minded and unstable."*[286]

So, what is doubt?

Doubt is unbelief, rejection, uncertainty, hesitation, skepticism, and a lack of conviction. *Has doubt ever stopped you?*

The first rule is to face the doubt head-on with belief. That's how Red McDaniel did it. Belief is the key to overcoming doubt. Jesus said, *"Anything is possible if a person believes."*[287]

Rule #2 - Take Action

Coach B tackled doubt at practice before game day. He showed us that the antidote for doubt is action. Compassion fuels courage, and when we step forward with courage despite the fear, doubt shrinks from a big, ugly horsefly to an inconsequential gnat.

Just like Joshua, who took command after Moses's passing, we must be ready to act. However, Joshua likely experienced serious doubt before his one-on-one with God, but that pep talk helped him face fear, and lead the Israelites.

The opposing force to doubt is faith in action. It's about belief and trust. This is where grit comes in.

James declares that faith without works is dead. It's not enough to simply believe—faith must be paired with action to be meaningful. Likewise, faith without imagination is equally lifeless; both must be actively pursued. True hope comes from combining faith, imagination, and action.

Like Joshua, recognize the importance of grit. Faith is measured not by our hope, but by the action we take to pursue that hope. Action turns self-doubt into self-doing. It leads our imagination to discover triumph. If you struggle with action, review chapter 7 again to explore how curiosity can compel you to act.

Rule #3 - Believe in Successful Outcomes

Zig Ziglar once said, *"Always remember that your present situation is not your final destination. The best is yet to come."*[288] Believing in successful outcomes was something I saw in Coach B.

In his day job, Coach B served as the speechwriter for Secretary of Defense Caspar Weinberger, who served under Ronald Reagan. I remember several practices where Coach B leveraged his speech-writing skills to inspire us.

Just days before we faced our toughest opponent, he gave a pep talk that essentially exorcised our doubt. He pulled on a thread of belief, transforming doubt into the conviction that we would win. The following Sunday, we won 3-1.

Beliefs drive behavior. It's rooted in faith, while behavior is grounded in grit. The measure of resilience—of faith and grit—are the 3Cs. Master those, and resilience becomes our ally.

Over time, I've learned that doubt is merely a figment of our imagination. It holds no power unless we harbor and feed it. Yet, how often do we let it take hold?

Remember, the antidote to doubt is action, fueled by hope. Hope is about believing that you can. Learning happens by doing. Doing is what eliminates doubt. If we don't act on hope, doubt can fester and grow like cancer. But when we believe in successful outcomes and act on that, hope comes alive.

The steps are simple; go, act, and bring hope with you. Because when we believe we can, we're already halfway there!

Rule #4 - Allow Discipline to Shape You

While we can minimize doubt by bringing hope with us, resilience doesn't come without challenges. But what if we learn to see the challenges as a means of discipline that gives direction? These challenges are the learning lessons.

I remember Coach B possessing something rare—gentle discipline. He respected all his players. He often took the time to get to know us individually. He rarely punished us by having us run suicides.

Instead, he elevated us with discipline by adding more elements of competition at practice. This connected us, stretched us, and prepared us.

The idea of discipline takes me back to when I was a kid. I remember I didn't always obey the rules. I was a curious mischief maker. When I did something wrong—really wrong—where I broke the rules meant to protect me and those around me, I would be reprimanded.

Like any kid, I hated getting punished. But the discipline I received didn't scar me for life. It helped shape me. Discipline is a form of course correction.

Walking in faith often involves receiving course corrections that get us to where we need to go. Discipline allows us to learn; that's why we need grit.

I remember my nephew got a nasty burn when he was a year old that sent him to the emergency room. He had reached for a hot tea kettle that spilled on him. The pain of that burn was far worse than the gentle slap of a hand that my sister wished she could have administered beforehand to alert him of danger. Discipline is preferred over pain.

Jim Rohn states, *"Discipline is the bridge between goals and accomplishment."*[289] It's a course correction to steer us in the right direction.

Remember, *"There is no effort without error or shortcoming."* Think of the challenge as discipline. The best, lean in and learn from the error or shortcoming?

The book of Proverbs in the Bible offers this insight:

> *"Do not despise the Lord's discipline, and*
> *do not resent his rebuke,*
> *because the Lord disciplines those he loves,*
> *as a father the son he delights in."*[290]

Let discipline make us stronger!

Rule #5 - Look for Wisdom

We didn't win all our games. But Coach B took those defeats and turned them into learning lessons, which then became leading lessons. Discipline leads to wisdom, but we must actively seek it.

Part of what Coach B did was help us reflect on alternative scenarios—what we could have done differently or better. His approach wasn't about criticizing our effort; it was about sharpening our focus.

One of my favorite passages in the Bible about gaining wisdom is found in the book of James:

> *"Consider it pure joy, my brothers and sisters, whenever you face trials of many kinds, because you know that the testing of your faith produces perseverance. Let perseverance finish its work so that you may be mature and complete, not lacking anything."*[291]

James continues:

> *"If any of you lacks wisdom, you should ask God, who gives generously to all without finding fault, and it will be given to you."*[292]

When we experience discipline, we should recognize there's something to learn from it. Experience is like a 4K streaming service to wisdom.

> *"Blessed are those who find wisdom, those who gain understanding, for she is more profitable than silver and yields better returns than gold."*[293]

Those who embrace the *Face the Mountain* mindset start to see the opportunities and strategies—what I call downloads. By using our experience and imagination, we learn how to pivot during the pain points.

Seek wisdom—*experienced knowledge*—as it is key to receiving these insights. That is why we should value having mentors in our life.

Rule #6 - Declare Dependence

Coach B taught us something else invaluable: resilience without reliance on one another leads to isolation. No man should feel alone in the arena. A team plays stronger together, and dependence on each other is paramount. We learned the importance of leaning on one another.

When it comes to dependence, there are two essential choices:

1) Rely on people we trust

2) Rely on a God who is always trustworthy

Sometimes, we think we can make it on our own. This is where our imagination can trip us up. Imagination is the portal to one of two things: worst-case scenarios or best-case scenarios. When we feel alone, the worst-case scenarios tend to take up residence in our minds. Our imagination may also lead us to play the comparison game, but comparison is an act of violence against ourselves.[294] Don't go there. That's not good faith. You are YOU—and there's no one else like you. Believe. Be you! But also find others who want to help you!

The best way to build confidence is to lean on those who believe in you. The belief others have in you is a gift to be received and accepted. If someone believes in you, then that's permission for you to believe in yourself.

The scriptures show that God, as a mentor and shepherd, believes in us. What is needed in reciprocation is our declaration of dependence on God. This means believing and trusting in Him. We can see this in David, Daniel, Ruth, and many other figures in the Bible. God was a source of trust, strength, and wisdom. What if He was the same for us?

One reminder I use to symbolize my dependence is an old U.S. coin. Occasionally, I rub my fingers on the inscription that says, *"In God We Trust."* It serves as a reminder of the source of my faith, assuring me that I'm not alone. Through faith and grit, I know that tomorrow will come. It's the *belief* that the same force that put the planets in motion is still on the job.

In the book of Luke, Jesus offers this advice:

> *"Do not worry about your life, what you will eat; or about your body, what you will wear. For life is more than food, and the body more than clothes."*[295]

As he continues speaking in this text, Jesus might be covering all Five Levels of Belief. He shares about the birds of the air, how God provides them with food and clothes the grass of the field. Then he asks some questions.

> *"How much more valuable you are than birds! Who of you by worrying can add a single hour to your life? Since you cannot do this very little thing, why do you worry about the rest? You of little faith!"*[296]

Jesus is trying to shore up what we believe. The response that he's looking for is our declaration of dependence and trust in God. What better source to depend on than the Creator of the universe?

The phrase *"In God We Trust"* first appeared on regimental banners in 1748, thanks to Benjamin Franklin's service in supplying mottos for a number of volunteer militia groups.[297] *"In God We Trust"* is a declaration of dependence—not independence.

I am reminded of a song by Grammy award-winning artist Steven Curtis Chapman entitled *Declaration of Dependence*.[298] Check out the lyrics:

> *"Now just the other day*
> *I overheard a flower talking to the sky*
> *He said, 'You know that I would be nothing without You'*
> *He said, 'You give me rain,*
> *you give the sun a place to shine*
> *You're everything that*
> *my whole existence comes down to'*
> *And then the flower started singing a song*
> *Before I knew it, I was singing along*
> *And we sang*
> *This is my declaration of dependence*
> *This is my declaration of my need."*

It's a catchy tune that triggers the imagination, but the second verse grabs my attention:

> *"Now, let me say that I'm the kind of guy*
> *who wants to do it all myself*
> *Don't want to ask for help,*
> *Don't like to stop for directions,*
> *But in reality, I'm nothing on my own*
> *It's by God's grace alone*
> *that I can make this confession."*[299]

The second verse highlights our human struggle for self-reliance, yet true strength comes from embracing our need for support. You and I were made for dependency; we don't have to climb the mountains alone. Faith means relying on something greater than ourselves. Grit means go!

Jesus encourages us to ask for help, seek what we need, and knock for the doors to open.[300] So, ask yourself, *Am I using my faith and grit? Why or why not?* Notice how much more confident we are when we know we are not alone. This confidence frees us up to develop compassion, and let our compassion draw others to us.

Rule #7 - Renew Your Mind

I mentioned earlier that Coach B would give us his pregame speech at practice rather than on game day. What he was doing was reshaping our minds when we practiced—not waiting for game day. By pulling on a thread of belief, he could extract us from our doubt and give us evidence of our faith in our abilities beforehand. That was huge. That gave us grit.

When game day arrived, we already knew we had what it took to do our best—we just needed to play the game the way we had practiced.

In my book *IMAGINE*, I discuss the importance of being *"transformed by the renewing of [our] mind."*[301] This element of imagination is a crucial part of resilience. What we think shapes who we are and the world around us. It's not a one-and-done event; like practice, it requires ongoing commitment and continual thinking.

Consider these quotes from some of the wisest people who ever walked the planet.

- *"For as he thinks in his heart, so is he."* – Solomon [302]

- *"The world as we have created it is a process of our thinking."* – Einstein [303]

- *"We become what we think about."* – Nightingale [304]

- *"Our lives are always moving in the direction of our strongest thoughts. What we think shapes who we are."* – Groeschel [305]

- *"What you're thinking is what you're becoming."* – Ali[306]

Great thinkers like these recognize that our thoughts matter. We must make wise choices to stay true to our beliefs.

The Four-Choice Outlook

We typically make one of four choices about how we see ourselves:

1. We see ourselves as not quite good enough.
2. We see ourselves as average, like everyone else.
3. We see ourselves as better than others.
4. We see ourselves as someone who can add value.

Which of these choices do you tend to subscribe to? Let's explore each of these tendencies.

1. We see ourselves as not quite good enough.

The first choice occurs when we see ourselves getting the short end of the stick. This is victim thinking. You feel beaten and bruised, often accompanied by negative self-talk or self-pity. This mindset can erode our self-esteem, making it difficult to believe in our abilities and potential.

Here are some common signs:

- You have lingering regrets about the past.

- You are pessimistic about the future or struggle to see the good around you.

- You experience a lack of motivation, strained relationships, and increased anxiety and stress.

- You develop perfectionist tendencies, pass up growth opportunities, or limit your vision for the future.

When this happens, our faith and imagination are at their lowest—but we don't have to stay there. Choose to see the good. Recognize that every day is a new day with fresh opportunities. Give yourself grace. Start with one simple goal to set the tone for the day.

The only day that truly matters is the present. Make it count.

2. We see ourselves as average, like everyone else.

The second choice occurs when we allow other people's perceptions to shape our reality. For instance, we might silently rely on the approval of others to validate our thinking—or our actions. *But what happens when we don't receive the affirmation we crave?*

Here's what can occur:

- Our faith can be shaken, and our imagination may limit us rather than lift us.

- Seeing ourselves as average can dampen our motivation, leading to complacency.

- It can cause us to overlook growth opportunities, negatively impact our self-esteem, and foster feelings of inadequacy.

- This mindset can trap us in a cycle of comparison, keeping us from setting ambitious goals and realizing our full potential.

- It can lead to stagnation in both our personal and professional lives.

Instead of falling into this trap, what if we embrace our unique strengths and strive for excellence? This approach can lead to a more fulfilling and successful life. But be cautious—choice 3 is just around the corner.

3. We see ourselves as better than others.

The third choice reflects pride, and slips us into the social comparison trap. This is when our self-worth is driven by how we think we stack up against others.

Check the signs:

- ☐ Do you constantly seek approval?

- ☐ Do you feel the need to prove yourself and push others to adopt your point of view?

If so, recognize this may eventually alienate you from others. Here's what might happen:

- Viewing ourselves (or our ideas) as superior can breed bitterness.

- It fosters a mentality of comparison and competition rather than one of growth and collaboration.

- Constant comparison can lead to feelings of inadequacy and resentment, eroding our sense of self-worth and contentment.

- It strains relationships, as others may feel judged or diminished by our attitude. This further isolates us and compounds bitterness.

In this state, our faith isn't necessarily a strength because our ego gets in the way. While our imagination may be active, it could also deceive us. Pride has tripped up humankind since the beginning, but what if we exchanged comparison for compassion? This leads us to choice 4.

4. We see ourselves as someone who can add value.

The fourth choice sets us up for real success, which is significance. We should have compassion for ourselves and recognize how God sees us, believes in us, and blesses us despite our imperfections. Let's be affirmed in who we are while remaining open to growth. We should also see others as people of value, and serve them.

When we choose to serve others and multiply value, several positive outcomes can occur:

- We experience greater fulfillment and build stronger relationships.

- Our motivation increases as we see the positive effects of our service, leading to personal growth and a positive ripple effect within our community.

Serving others not only improves our mental health but allows us to create a lasting impact. Our imagination will uplift us, and resilience will be a defining quality of who we are.

Discover What God Believes About You

A powerful tool that has helped me is using "I Am" statements grounded in scripture—affirmations that reflect how God sees us. Below are thirty-one "I Am" statements designed to strengthen the 3Cs of Resilience. Let these words shape our self-perception and encourage us to embrace the compassion God has for us.

Table 5 – "I Am" Affirmations

1.	I am not alone.	2 Timothy 4:17
2.	I am loved.	Psalm 57:10
3.	I am blessed.	Jeremiah 17:7
4.	I am able to enjoy life and peace.	Romans 8:6
5.	I am empowered with wisdom.	1 Corinthians 2:13
6.	I am bold.	Hebrews 4:16
7.	I am strong.	Psalm 46:1
8.	I am prepared for the journey.	Proverbs 3:6
9.	I am equipped to bear fruit.	John 15:5
10.	I am able to ask God to direct me.	Psalm 139:23-24
11.	I am hopeful.	Psalm 40:7
12.	I am made new.	Romans 6:4
13.	I am created for a purpose.	2 Timothy 2:20-21
14.	I am a voice to encourage others.	1 Corinthians 14:3
15.	I am on God's team and can't be cut.	Romans 8:39
16.	I am complete.	Colossians 2:10
17.	I am saved.	Luke 2:11
18.	I am more than a conqueror.	Romans 8:37
19.	I am protected in times of trouble.	Psalm 9:9
20.	I am rested.	Matthew 11:28
21.	I am an agent of change.	Ephesians 2:10
22.	I am fearfully and wonderfully made.	Psalm 139:1
23.	I am approved by God.	2 Corinthians 10:18
24.	I am able to share truth with others.	Colossians 1:28-29
25.	I am qualified to teach others.	2 Timothy 2:2
26.	I am a child of God.	1 John 3:1
27.	I am free.	Galatians 5:1
28.	I am able to walk in the light.	John 8:12
29.	I am created to glorify God.	Isaiah 43:7
30.	I am on the right path.	Proverbs 3:6
31.	I am able to face the mountain.	Psalm 121:1

Which "I am" statements can you lean on for yourself today?

Action Steps

This chapter emphasizes the importance of practicing compassion in our work. It shows compassion not only builds resilience but also enhances our competence and courage. By nurturing a compassionate heart and a confident mindset, we are better prepared to meet challenges. To fully embrace compassion, consider these three action steps:

1. *Reflect and prepare with purpose*

Acknowledge challenges as opportunities for growth rather than permanent setbacks. Reflect on past experiences and identify a specific action to better equip yourself for future challenges. This step is akin to preparing for "the mountain" ahead, building resilience through anticipation and readiness.

2. *Envision and embody the "I Am" values*

As part of the preparation, contemplate the kind of person you aspire to be and the future you envision. Focus on embodying the "I Am" values. Picture the best version of yourself, shaped by these values, and let this vision guide your actions and decisions.

3. *Show compassion "Anyway"*

After two steps of preparation, it's time to act. One of the most impactful figures of intentional compassion was Mother Teresa. Though she has passed, we can still learn much from her example.

Mother Teresa was known for her compassion, especially for the children in Calcutta. She displayed a powerful poem of intentionality on the wall of her home titled *"Do It Anyway,"* reflecting her intentional mindset.[307] Let this poem serve as encouragement to practice compassion, even in the face of adversity.

Do It Anyway

attributed to Saint Mother Teresa of Calcutta

People are often unreasonable,
irrational, and self-centered.
Forgive Them Anyway.

If you are kind,
people may accuse you of selfish, ulterior motives.
Be Kind Anyway.

If you are successful, you will win some
unfaithful friends and some genuine enemies.
Succeed Anyway.

If you are honest and sincere
people may deceive you.
Be Honest and Sincere Anyway.

What you spend years creating,
others could destroy overnight.
Create Anyway.

If you find serenity and happiness,
some may be jealous.
Be Happy Anyway.

The good you do today,
will often be forgotten.
Do Good Anyway.

Give the best you have,
and it will never be enough.
Give Your Best Anyway.

In the final analysis,
it is between you and God.
It Was Never Between You and Them Anyway.[308]

Let us be inspired by Mother Teresa's example and choose to respond to life's circumstances with intentional compassion. No matter the reactions of others or the challenges we face, let us commit to kindness, honesty, and perseverance. Resilience is the work of faith and grit!

EPILOGUE –
SPEAK TO THE MOUNTAIN

"It is not the mountain we conquer but ourselves."
– Sir Edmund Hillary

D o you recall the story I told at the beginning about the landslide that almost brought me down?

Full confession: I wish I could say I followed Tom Hemingway's advice after that near-death experience. He told me that I was on borrowed time, and to make the most of it. But the truth is, the fall rattled me. I became timid and apprehensive. In the weeks, months, and even years that followed, my zeal for life took a back seat. I let it become a season of winter.

Looking back now, I see someone who put dreams on pause. My "before-and-after" mindset radically changed.

Before the fall, I was adventurous. I wanted to climb all the fourteeners in Colorado. After the fall, I was content to view those mountains from a distance. *"They look good right there,"* I'd tell myself.

Before the fall, I dreamed of attending the Air Force Academy or Naval Academy and serving my country. After the fall, I chose the easier road—attending a traditional school and sticking to the status quo. *"There's a reason why people don't go to a military academy,"* I rationalized.

Before the fall, I aspired to be a professional athlete. After the fall, I settled for sitting on the couch, watching others compete. *"Who am I kidding? Only a few ever make it,"* I convinced myself.

Before the fall, I had big ideas and bold aspirations. After the fall, I second-guessed every idea and questioned every dream. *"Who says that you can? You'll fall. You'll fail. Better to play it safe."* I became my own worst critic.

I can't tell you how many years this mindset stole from me. For a while, I followed the script others set instead of living life fully. *Why?*

Because I was afraid—afraid of falling again. I figured the status quo was safer. I didn't want to blaze my own trail. It was only during my last semester of college, four years later, that I started to dream again.

Like many of you, I've faced unexpected challenges that changed the course of my life. But I learned to get back up, show compassion for myself, and rebuild using the 3Cs of Resilience—Competence, Courage, and Compassion. I'm still a work in progress, but I feel compelled to share these lessons with you.

I wrote this book to offer a message of hope. It's time to stop sitting on the sidelines. Fear's greatest power lies in making us hesitate, keeping us from taking action. That's where regret sets in. But hope isn't found in the past—it lies in the opportunities ahead, often disguised as mountains.

Remember, you are the one in the arena. Your place is not with those "who neither know victory nor defeat."[309] There is only one choice: *face the mountain!*

Sir Edmund Hillary – *Master Climber*

Of all the people on the planet who you think would conquer the tallest mountain in the world, you probably would have never picked a beekeeper from New Zealand. But that was Edmund Hillary. Known for his integrity, modesty, determination, and service to others, Hillary became the first man to climb Mount Everest, which he did in 1953.

Edmund Hillary climbed eleven different peaks of over twenty thousand feet in his lifetime, an astounding achievement. After one particularly difficult attempt, he had to retreat down the mountain. But instead of admitting defeat, he made a profound statement, speaking to the mountain directly:

> *"I will come again and conquer you*
> *because as a mountain you can't grow,*
> *but as a human, I can!"[310]*

Sure enough, Hillary trained himself to look at challenges as opportunities. He recognized that to climb a mountain—or face a challenge head-on—requires a growth mindset and unwavering belief. We can't make the climb unless we believe. Belief is about faith; climbing is about grit.

When Hillary finally summited Mount Everest, it gave others permission to believe they could do the same. He changed the world. What once was impossible became possible. Over eleven thousand people have now climbed Everest, proving that the 3Cs can break limiting beliefs. The key is to be consistent over time.

How the 3Cs Fuel Resilience

Let's revisit the Theory of Resiliency to understand the role of time:

$$I = 3C^T$$

In this equation, "*I*" stands for *impact*—the change we can make. The "3C" represents Competence, Courage, and Compassion—three measurable components of faith and grit. "*T*" represents *time.*

Another way to look at this equation is to expand the 3Cs:

$$I = (c_1 \times c_2 \times c_3)^T$$

By expanding the 3Cs:

- **C1 (Competence):**
    - Equips us to face challenges with confidence.
- **C2 (Courage):**
    - Equips us to act bravely despite fear.
- **C3 (Compassion):**
    - Equips us to support ourselves and others through adversity.

The consistent application of these over time is what creates lasting impact and empowers us to change the world.

The Power to Change the World

"The Power to Change the World" isn't just about grand actions or monumental achievements; it's about the consistent, resilient steps we take in the face of our own mountains. The 3Cs of Resilience—Competence, Courage, and Compassion—powered by faith and grit, give us this transformative power.

Every mountain we face—whether in our personal lives, careers, or relationships—requires faith, grit, and the determination to keep climbing, no matter the obstacles. Resilience is about growing stronger with each step, discovering deeper purpose, and inspiring others along the way.

When we face our mountains with courage and determination, we transform ourselves and create ripples of change in the world around us. The power to change the world lies in the small, intentional actions fueled by hope and unwavering belief. As we rise, we light a path for others. This is the essence of facing the mountain: pushing forward with resilience unlocks the power within us to conquer our challenges and inspire change far beyond ourselves.

Build with Words

Nelson Mandela changed the world by first transforming himself. In the movie *Invictus* directed by Clint Eastwood, Mandela (portrayed by Morgan Freeman), and Francois Pienaar, the captain of the South Africa's rugby team (portrayed by Matt Damon), came from opposite social classes and backgrounds. However, both men shared common values, including a deep love for their country.

As the newly elected president of South Africa, Mandela wanted to make good on his campaign promise to unite the country and help end racial division. The sport of rugby caught his eye as a potential way to achieve that goal.

With the upcoming Rugby World Cup, Mandela seized on the opportunity and collaborated with Pienaar. They discussed what it took to face challenges and overcome struggles. In a reflective moment, Mandela recalled his time in prison and what sustained him during those difficult years:

> *"On Robben Island, when things got very bad, I found inspiration in a poem. A Victorian poem. [They were] just words. But they helped me to stand when all I wanted to do was to lie down."*[311]

He referred to William Ernest Henley's poem *Invictus. Invictus* is Latin for "unconquered." This poem reminds us of the strength we can have in the midst of adversity.

The last two lines of the poem particularly inspired Mandela:

"I am the master of my fate,
I am the captain of my soul."[312]

These words reminded Mandela that all of us are responsible for our actions despite our circumstances. Faith is important, but faith not acted upon is just a wish. This poem motivated Mandela to be resilient. It reminded him to stay sharp and alive despite the torment of prison. Over time, it shaped his character and the values that enabled him to lead with Competence, Courage, and Compassion—the 3Cs.

Pienaar, the rugby captain, also emphasized the power of words. He spoke of how the words from a good song could inspire him and his team right before a match.[313] As a sports fan, I love this thought. Words power the 3Cs.

Go Fast. Go Far!

In my research for this book, I discovered that the song Pienaar and his teammates connected with is called *Shosholoza,* a Ndebele folk song from Zimbabwe sung by the mixed tribes of gold miners in South Africa. Over time, it has become a song of hope and encouragement, embraced and sung by many, including Peter Gabriel, Pete Seeger, John Edmond, the Soweto Gospel Choir, and the South African rugby team. The song is considered by many to be South Africa's second national anthem.

The word *Shosholoza,* which is also the first word of each verse and the chorus, means *"to go forward, go fast, and make way for the next man."*[314] Its sound, *"sho sho,"* as it's sung, is reminiscent of a steam train and evokes a sense of urgency and progress. The second phrase is *kulezo ntaba,* meaning *"on those mountains."* Together, they are sung in harmony:

"Shosholoza kulezo ntaba."
"Go fast, go far, on those mountains."[315]

The profound meaning is a rallying cry to *face the mountain.* Words matter. They tell a story and can show a path. In his foreword for Kevin Hall's brilliant book *Aspire,* Stephen Covey shares this insight about the power of words:

"Words contain an inherent power, a force capable of lighting one's paths and hoped-for horizons. Used correctly and positively, words are the first building blocks for success and inner peace; they provide the vision and

focus that show the way to growth and contribution. Used incorrectly and negatively, they are capable of undermining even the best of intentions."[316]

Words, like our imagination, can either lift us or limit us. Sometimes, just one word can provide the foundation we need to weather the storm.

I encourage you to take a moment to think about the words that are meaningful to you. Consider words like *passion, hope,* and *dream,* which were used by leaders like Mandela and Martin Luther King, Jr., to inspire and mobilize others toward their goals of freedom, justice, and equality. *What inspires and motivates you?*

In 2018, five years after Mandela passed, the United Nations was gifted a life-size bronze statue of Nelson Mandela from the Republic of South Africa. Upon receiving the gift, UN Secretary-General Antonio Guterres remarked:

"Nelson Mandela embodied the highest values—peace, forgiveness, compassion, and human dignity. He was a champion for all people in his words and in his actions. He was willing to fight and die for the ideals he held so dear."[317]

This eulogy prompts me to ask: What values will others attribute to us when they look back on our lives? How will we *face the mountains?* Will our actions inspire others to change the world?

Speak to the Mountain

Competence, Courage, and Compassion require time and commitment. *Are you patient on your climb?*

As you *face the mountain,* what do you believe? Does it scare you and make you retreat? Or does it compel you to keep trying?

Facing the mountain begins with belief. When we fall down, we get back up. *Why?* Because we believe. Belief never stops. Belief means our story is not over.

Often, we call out for help and ask God for strength. There's nothing wrong with that, but Mark Batterson shares a powerful shift in perspective:

"There comes a moment when you must quit talking to God about the mountain . . . and start talking to the mountain about your God."[318]

It's time to turn the tide. Speak to the mountain. Let it know you're coming!

Take the Summit

Reaching the summit requires belief in ourselves and others. No one changes the world without struggle. It's belief that keeps us going.

Faith and grit fuel our journey. Our ability to emerge from the valley and conquer the mountain lies not just in hope, but in trust in something greater than ourselves. Faith and grit remind us that we're not alone.

Jesus articulated this concept beautifully:

"If your faith is as small as a mustard seed, you can say to this mountain, 'Move from here to there,' and it will move. All things will be possible for you."[319]

Actor Jeremy Renner's story exemplifies resilience. After a near-fatal accident, he reflected on the power of belief with this social media post:

"Checking in with this thought. All of the obstacles, the problems, and failures are my allies of whom pour the foundation where my successes are built . . . to anyone who is struggling with failures or overwhelming obstacles, I wish and will upon you a powerful belief that you are not alone . . . and collectively we can move MOUNTAINS!!!"[320]

Renner's words highlight how challenges form the bedrock of the 3Cs of Resilience—Competence, Courage, and Compassion. Moreover, belief is the cornerstone of this resilience. We are not alone in our struggles; together, belief makes the impossible achievable.

Jesus acknowledged life's storms, but also shared a message of hope, reminding us that it's not all gloom and doom:

"I have told you all this so that you will have peace of heart and mind. Here on earth, you will have many trials and sorrows; but cheer up, for I have overcome the world."[321]

Every challenge is a reminder that each new day is a gift. How will you use it?

Embrace the *Face the Mountain* mindset and dare greatly. With faith and grit, the 3Cs of Resilience become our compass. This compass gives us permission to speak to the mountain. When we move, the mountain moves. That's the power of resilience.

Resilience isn't just about conquering our own mountains; it's about inspiring others to conquer theirs. When we lead with resilience and navigate through the Five Levels of Belief, we don't just transform our lives—we ignite change in the lives of others.

So, *face the mountain*. Take that step forward with faith and grit. It's the steady steps that change the world.

Acknowledgments

I couldn't have shared the stories in this book without the influence of my mom and dad and the impact of my wife.

Even though it's been over fifteen years since his passing, I miss my dad greatly. His advice and prayers saved me a time or two.

My mom has been a stalwart, taking on the prayer focus, and has been an encouragement to my incredible family. Thank you, Mom, for being, well, Mom and Grandma!

My wife Barb, whom I call Valentine, she has been the blessing of blessings in my life. I've seen her climb the figurative mountain a time or two, and there have been some tough ones. But she keeps getting back up. She is my inspiration. Valentine, I love you. Let's keep climbing.

Tom Hemingway passed long ago, but I still need to acknowledge him and thank his family for allowing me to share a little bit of his life. It was a short mentorship, but clearly, he impacted me. It's a reminder that teens and young adults need mentors. I had one. I had several. Parents are key, but there needs to be people outside of the family, too. We all need a Tom Hemingway or Coach B in our lives. As you are reading this, consider who you can be a mentor.

I have an army of mentors in the books I read. Some I know personally, some I have not yet connected with, but through their writings, they have connected with me. If you are an author, keep writing. You never know who you might influence and what impact you might make.

I want to thank my SimVentions family. I'm coming up on twenty-five years. Together, we've climbed some incredible mountains. I am so proud of every one of you. Thanks for being part of the SimV team. Together, we're better. We exist to honor others. Let's keep doing that.

I want to thank my Wednesday morning accountability group, a.k.a. *the Thought Leader Jedis*. Each month, it's a new book. Each week, it's a fresh discussion, and each year, it's a few days out in the Rockies facing the mountains for a yearly reset. I am blessed by each of you.

I want to thank the incredible CADRE community of entrepreneurs and leaders for their dedication to business growth, personal development, and connection. A special thanks to my Cadre committee, who continually help me step out of my comfort zone and into the potential zone.

Special thanks to Kari Ann Hawthorne, for her incredible diligence in combing through the book. I couldn't have asked for a better editor. Thanks also to Daniel Hammond, Joe Dutkiewicz and Mike Lightner for the content review of the manuscript for this book. You helped me get to a higher elevation on this journey. Also, I would like to give a shout-out to my coach, Mike Harbour. Thanks for all you did to help me chart my flight.

Next, I want to thank Doug, Barry, Richard, my friend Bill, and my two sons, who help me get back up whenever I need it. Thank you for always being a call or text away.

Lastly, I want to thank God for giving me the nudge to write this book. God, I see what You did. You let me get *IMAGINE* done first and face a few mountains of my own so that I could write the book You wanted all along. You're pretty clever! Thank You for giving me a passion to write. Writing is my release and way to align. When I write, I can feel Your whisper. My prayer is that these words lift us and remind us to be strong and courageous, knowing we're here for a reason. Keep reminding us that You are always with us.

This leads me to the Climber's Prayer.

APPENDIX A –
THE CLIMBER'S PRAYER

L ife is full of challenges that test our resolve. One key lesson from The Hook is that no one should climb alone—life is meant to be shared. We find strength and courage in those around us and in God who guides us. I offer this prayer for those on the climb—a guide for facing the mountain head-on. It reminds us to embrace Competence, Courage, and Compassion, and to lean on each other for strength as we rise to the challenge.

THE CLIMBER'S PRAYER

by Paul Gustavson

In the shadow of the towering peak, we stand.
Oh Mountain, our God guides us with a steady hand.
He grants us Competence, wisdom to see,
As storms approach, our faith calms the sea.

In times of trial, Courage becomes our light;
It's not just faith, it's also the grit to fight.
With boldness, we face the daunting climb;
If we stumble, we rise, leaving doubt behind.

Compassion and empathy fill our soul;
Our mission is to serve, and honor is the goal.
Teach us to listen, to help, and lend a hand,
To be a beacon, a friend, lifting what souls we can.

These three Cs, we humbly pray:
Competence, Courage, and Compassion to guide the way.
God, grant us strength to climb and carry on;
With resolve, we face the mountain, steady and strong.

For all who hear this call to act,
Together let's rise and never look back.
We climb with resilience, beyond the range,
Harnessing the power within, our world to change.

And so, we stand—ready to face the mountain.

APPENDIX B –
THE FIVE MOUNTAINS

T o achieve a worthy goal, we must face a mountain to climb. In this book, we've shared stories and strategies for navigating challenges and impacting the world. For the resilient, each climb can lead to success or significance. Often, the best views and impacts stem from the toughest climbs.

As an analogy to life's challenges and our journey, let's consider the five classes of mountains we might encounter. While none of them are easy, each offers a rewarding gift.

Class 1 – The Hike

Class 1 mountains can be significant. But the good news is that others have tackled them. They're not insurmountable. There will be changes in elevation, but there is also a marked trail. As long as you can walk, you can do it.

As tall as it is, consider Mount Kilimanjaro in Africa. It's a Class 1 climb. In less than one week's time, you can summit this mountain by taking a clearly marked trail. You just need to be in reasonably good shape and have the right gear, water, food, good weather, and ample time.

Class 1 Mountains are analogous to what we face in a week's time in life. Nothing in life is less than a Class 1 mountain. The key is to get up when we fall. Just keep climbing! The summit is there for those who keep going. The toughest enemy is fatigue. Even if the storms come, we can reposition and wait it out. Patience and persistence are the keys.

Class 2 – The Scramble

These mountains present more challenges than Class 1 climbs, often requiring hikers to use their hands for scrambling up or down. States like Colorado and California offer many Class 2 climbs, which typically involve easy scrambling and non-technical terrain.

These hikes attract those looking for a step up from standard trails, offering a bit more challenge. While they can be strenuous and weather conditions should be monitored, they remain accessible for many hikers.

Class 2 mountains are analogous to unscheduled surprises that come our way on any given day. Sometimes, we need to scramble to continue the climb. Sometimes, we just need to grin and bear it, giving everything we've got.

Class 3 – The Advanced Scramble

These types of mountains are tough. The pitch on a Class 3 can be challenging, and footing may slip. This is a hike with exposed scrambling where a fall could be fatal. Old Ragged Mountain in Virginia, Sahale Peak in Washington and Longs Peak in Colorado represent Class 3 climbs. The Hook mentioned in the prologue would be considered a Class 3 climb.

Class 3 mountains are analogous to what a leader of any team faces when pursuing challenges. The scrambles sometimes seem endless. We find ourselves pivoting, shifting, and straining just to keep up. In these situations, it's hard to find a moment of rest. One slip might be fatal. But the good news is that we can condition ourselves to weather the storms on a Class 3 mountain.

Class 4 – The Climb

These types of mountains are extremely challenging. They are more than just a hike or a scramble; consider the difficulty of Maroon Peak in Colorado, or the Summit Pyramid in Washington. These ascents include steep, exposed climbing, and yet, often a rope isn't used. While confidence is essential on these mountains, overconfidence can be deadly. One slip or fall can be catastrophic.

Class 4 mountains are analogous to what a leader faces when storms come unexpectedly. Sometimes the best way to climb this type of mountain is to climb back down and readjust. Faith will feel tested, and resilience will be revealed. This is where pressure transitions from coal into diamonds.

Stay the course. Remember, faith without grit is incomplete—it's like having a vision without action or a dream without determination. Grit is the catalyst that transforms belief into reality, turning hope into accomplishment. Without it, faith remains an unfulfilled promise. Together, faith and grit can move mountains and overcome any obstacle.

Class 5 – The Technical Climb

These types of mountains appear nearly impossible. This is more extreme climbing. Rope and belaying are essential. Most mountains you would summit in Yosemite National Park offer Class 5 climbs. The number of fatalities in Yosemite is about sixteen-to-seventeen persons per year on these mountains. Mount Everest, the tallest mountain on the planet, is Class 5. It is estimated that more than three hundred people have died on Mount Everest since Sir Edmund Hillary climbed it in 1953.

Class 5 mountains are analogous to both our best and worst days as a leader. The storms and terrain can get bad, but the views can be spectacular. The best way to climb this mountain is with clarity, calmness, and courage. It's realizing we need help from other people through the challenge. Branch Rickey and Jackie Robinson, who we discussed in chapter 4, needed each other. Neither one of them could have climbed that mountain alone. The key to this climb is to remember we have others to help us. Use the ropes of connection. Look to pull each other up.

Class 5 isn't just about reaching the summit; it's about the journey there and back. While it won't be easy, I've heard that nothing is more rewarding than climbing a Class 5. The first person to reach the summit is remembered forever, but those who help others along the way leave a lasting legacy.

APPENDIX C – THE RESILIENCE CHECKLIST

Every mountaineer needs a checklist. The chapters in this book can be boiled down into four key checkpoints that will guide you with resilience.

Table 6 – Your Resilience Checklist

☐ **BASELINE CHECKPOINT**	What mountains am I facing? Where am I right now on this journey? How am I doing with the 3Cs of resilience? Where can I improve?
☐ **COMPETENCE CHECKPOINT**	It's about knowing the job, and striving hard to learn it better.
- Anticipating Storms?	What potential challenges lie ahead? How's my mindset? Am I ready to face whatever comes my way?
- Building Beliefs?	What core beliefs guide me? How does my life reflect my values? At what "level" of faith am I living by?
- Committed to Duty?	What is my calling, and how do I serve it? What are my unique strengths? How do I show grit in my actions?
☐ **COURAGE CHECKPOINT**	It's about making the hard but right decisions.
- Asking, "Why Not?"	Do I choose courage as a deliberate act? What outcome do I hope for? What steps must I take to achieve it? Do my thoughts build me up, or tear me down?
- Being Curious?	Do I seek out new opportunities and challenges? What am I learning and discovering right now? Does my imagination inspire me, or limit me?
- Creating Calm?	How's my emotional intelligence (EQ)? Am I maintaining a calm attitude under pressure?

☐ **COMPASSION CHECKPOINT**	It's about caring for others.
- Acclimating?	Am I focused on what truly matters? Who are my trusted "sherpas" on this journey? How do I serve as a "sherpa" for others?
- Being Intentional?	Am I nurturing hope? In what ways? Do I practice empathy in my interactions? Are my words life-giving and constructive?
- Cultivating Care?	How am I cultivating care for myself and others? Who do I support, encourage, and uplift? What specific needs do I bring to prayer?
- Doing It Anyway?	Am I taking meaningful actions toward my goals? Do I believe in my ability to succeed? Do I support the potential of others? How do my actions reflect my compassion?

Use this checklist as a guide to help you and others *face the mountain*—so that together, we can change the world.

ABOUT THE AUTHOR

Paul Gustavson

Paul is a tech industry leader with a passion for innovation and the outdoors. He is the co-founder and CTO of *SimVentions*, which was established in 2000. *SimVentions* supports today's military and decision-makers with innovative engineering solutions and services. The *Virginia Chamber* and *Inc. Magazine* have recognized *SimVentions* as one of the best places to work.

As the CTO, Paul fosters innovation, contributes to the company's strategic vision, leads IR&D efforts, provides technical expertise, and participates in industry standards development. Paul is also the author of *IMAGINE*, *BREAKING AVERAGE*, *LEADERS PRESS ON*, and *SPEECH BLUEPRINT* and co-host of the *Breaking Average Podcast*. He is an active member of the simulation community.

You can connect with Paul at the following links:

- https://www.simventions.com (corporate)
- https://breakingaverage.com (personal)
- X: @PaulGustavson
- Instagram: @paul.gustavson

◆ ◆ ◆

Additional tools and resources are available at
FaceTheMtn.com

ENDNOTES

1. Teddy Roosevelt, *The Man in the Arena: Citizenship in a Republic*, April 23, 1910. The full speech is available at https://www.theodoreroosevelt.org/content.aspx?page_id=22&club_id=991271&module_id=339364.

2. Colonel Arthur J. Athens, *Leadership: What's Love Got to Do With It?* (Paper presented at 1/C Capstone Seminar, sponsored by The Vice Admiral James B. Stockdale Center for Ethical Leadership, U.S. Naval Academy, Annapolis, MD, January 11, 2008), 3.

Author's note: In my research for the story of the 3Cs from Tom Hemingway, I came across this white paper written by Colonel Athens. To me, it's the Holy Grail unlocking the source of the 3Cs that I learned when I was 17 years old. I reached out to Colonel Athens for his blessing to share this. Here is what he shared:

"The *What's Love Got to Do With It?* paper is actually a transcript of a presentation I made at the Naval Academy. And yes . . . Tom told me the story of the 3Cs many years ago. He was a dear friend and mentor. I'm confident Tom made a significant impact on your life . . . as he did for so many."

Since then, Colonel Athens has passed on the 3Cs to others, including his son before he set off to serve in our military. The story I recount in this book is clearly the one that Tom Hemingway shared with Art Athens. I wanted to honor that dialogue by presenting it to you. Thank you, Colonel Athens, for bringing this to the world and allowing me to share it in these pages.

3. Athens, 3; emphasis mine.

4. Athens, 3; emphasis mine.

5. Athens, 3; emphasis mine.

6. Athens, 3; emphasis mine.

7. Athens, 3; emphasis mine.

8. John 16:33 (New Living Translation).

9. Homer, *The Iliad,* https://www.goodreads.com/quotes/400731-the-roaring-seas-and-many-a-dark-range-of-mountains. *The Iliad* and *The Odyssey,* epics written by Homer, are the oldest surviving works of Greek literature. He composed them in the eighth century B.C. (750 B.C. for *The Iliad,* 720 B.C. for *The Odyssey*).

10. *The Lord of the Rings: The Two Towers,* directed by Peter Jackson (2002; Burbank, CA: New Line Cinema), Amazon Prime. Performances by Viggo Mortensen as Aragorn and Ian McKellen as Gandalf.

11. *The Two Towers*, Jackson.

12. J.R.R. Tolkien, https://www.goodreads.com/quotes/6565732-the-great-storm-is-coming-but-the-tide-has-turned.

13. *The Lord of the Rings: The Return of the King,* directed by Peter Jackson (2003; Burbank, CA: New Line Cinema), Amazon Prime.

14. Jeremy Schaap, *Triumph: The Untold Story of Jesse Owens and Hitler's Olympics* (Boston: Mariner Books, 2008).

15. Jesse Owens, https://www.goodreads.com/quotes/1018216-the-battles-that-count-aren-t-the-ones-for-gold-medals.

16. Jesse Owens, https://www.goodreads.com/quotes/563376-we-all-have-dreams-but-in-order-to-make-dreams.

17. *Faith.* The language data is provided by Oxford Languages, part of Oxford University Press, accessed via Google June 30, 2024, https://www.google.com/search?q=definition+faith.

18. A common definition for *faith* is found in chapter 11 of the book of Hebrews within the Bible. "Now faith is the assurance of things hoped for, the conviction of things not seen" (English Standard Version).

19. Ronald Reagan, *Remarks at the Annual National Prayer Breakfast*, February 3, 1983,https://www.reaganlibrary.gov/archives/speech/remarks-annual-national-prayer-breakfast-2.

20. Ronald Reagan, *Remarks at the Annual Convention of the National Religious Broadcasters*, January 31, 1983, https://www.reaganlibrary.gov/archives/speech/remarks-annual-convention-national-religious-broadcasters-0#.
Note: Centuries earlier, the apostle Paul made a similar remark in his letter to Timothy, who was an emerging leader. "All Scripture is inspired by God and is useful. . . . God uses it to PREPARE and EQUIP his people to do every good work." 2 Timothy 3:16-17 (New Living Translation); emphasis mine.

21. My teachers told us to show our work. They wanted more than the answer; they wanted to know the path we had taken to find the answer. That's what GRIT represents; it's showing the work.

22. Jim Rohn wrote a terrific book about the Four Seasons, titled *The Seasons of Life*, which explores the similarities between our lives and the changing seasons. His book is based on the parable of the sower and the reaper. What we do in one season impacts us in the next season.

23. Isaiah 40:30 (New International Version).

24. Genesis 3:19 (NIV).

25. Genesis 49:19 (NIV).

26. Jeremiah 30:7 (NIV).

27. Psalm 55:18 (NIV).

28. 2 Corinthians 4:8 (NIV).

29. John 16:33 (NLT).

30. Luke 1:37 (Amplified Bible, Classic Edition).

31. Alice in Wonderland, directed by Tim Burton (2010; Burbank, CA: Walt Disney Pictures/Walt Disney Studios Motion Pictures), Amazon Prime. Also see: Moment, "THE ONLY WAY TO ACHIEVE THE IMPOSSIBLE IS TO BELIEVE IT IS POSSIBLE | MOTIVATION," February 7, 2024, https://www.youtube.com/watch?v=oEEhjzXgFKo.

32. Adidas Advertisement, "Impossible is Nothing" campaign featuring Muhammad Ali, 2004. Note: Adidas also ran this commercial titled "The Long Run" in 2004 featuring Ali and other notable athletes (Zinedine Zidane, Laila Ali, David Beckham, Tracy McGrady, Ian Thorpe, Haile Gebrselassie and Maurice Green): Eric Allen, "BEST QUALITY** Muhammad Ali - Impossible Is Nothing (Adidas)," June 29, 2012, https://www.youtube.com/watch?v=AScl_l6GXLA.

33. John Acuff, *All It Takes Is a Goal* (Grand Rapids, MI: Baker Books, 2023). In this bestselling book, Acuff shares about three zones that we grapple with: The Comfort Zone, the Potential Zone, and the Chaos Zone. It's a terrific book that I recommend for goal setting.

34. Douglas Malloch, "*Good Timber*," 1922. For more on how this message can apply to your life, I encourage you to also pick up *Permission to Be Bold*, by Barbara Gustavson.

35. *42*, directed by Brian Helgeland (2013; Burbank, CA: Warner Bros.), Amazon Prime. The film stars Chadwick Boseman as Jackie Robinson and Harrison Ford as Branch Rickey. Note: The title of the movie is a reference to Robinson's jersey number, which was retired for all MLB teams in 1997.

36. *42*, Helgeland.

37. *42*, Helgeland.

38. *42*, Helgeland.

39. Teddy Roosevelt, *The Man in the Arena: Citizenship in a Republic*, April 23, 1910. The full speech is available at https://www.theodoreroosevelt.org/content.aspx?page_id=22&club_id=991271&module_id=339364.

40. I observed these 42 values in Branch Rickey and Jackie Robinson from the movie *42*. I also took the liberty to evaluate some of the other leadership characters that the actors played in the movies Air Force One, Indiana Jones, and Patriot Games for Harrison Ford, and Marshall and Black Panther for the late Chadwick Boseman.

41. *Ted Lasso*, written by Jason Sudeikis, Bill Lawrence, Brendan Hunt, and Joe Kelly, among others; Jason Sudeikis starred as Ted Lasso. Season One premiered on Apple TV+ on August 14, 2020, Season Two premiered July 23, 2021, Season Three premiered March 15, 2023.

42. *Ted Lasso*, Sudeikis.

43. Eleanor Roosevelt, https://www.goodreads.com/quotes/6358-the-future-belongs-to-those-who-believe-in-the-beauty.

44. Michael H. Connors and Peter W. Halligan, "Revealing the Cognitive Neuroscience of Belief," July 18, 2022, https://www.frontiersin.org/articles/10.3389/fnbeh.2022.926742/full.

45. Connors and Halligan, "Revealing the Cognitive Neuroscience of Belief."

46. Fu Che, personal conversation I had with him, April 2024.

47. Teddy Roosevelt, *The Man in the Arena*.
Author's note: This is one line from his speech that impacted me.

48. Philippians 4:8 (English Standard Version).

49. Paul Gustavson, *IMAGINE: The Surprising Truth about Hope and the 12 Powerful Ways to Invent the Future* (Fredericksburg, VA: LeadEdgePress, 2022), 15.

Author's note: The Oxford English Dictionary defines imagination as "the faculty or action of forming new ideas, images or concepts of external objects not present to the senses."

50. Paul Gustavson, *IMAGINE: The Surprising Truth about Hope and the 12 Powerful Ways to Invent the Future* (Fredericksburg, VA: LeadEdgePress, 2022), 90.

51. "Negative Thoughts and Brain Health/Amen Clinics," Sept. 16, 2020, https://www.amenclinics.com/blog/do-you-have-an-ant-infestation-in-your-head/.

52. Abraham H. Maslow (1943), "A Theory of Human Motivation," *Psychological Review,* 50(4), 370-96.

53. Author's note: The Five Levels of Belief emerged from my research for this book. As I explored our levels of belief tied to faith and grit, I began to see how they align with Maslow's Hierarchy of Needs. Specifically, each level of Maslow's needs offers a space that can be filled by the depth of our belief. I found this fascinating. My hope is that the Five Levels of Belief will provide clarity and guidance, helping us recognize that the challenges we face—reflective of our needs—can also fuel and strengthen our resilience.

54. "Maslow's Hierarchy of Needs, Scalable Vector Illustration Stock Vector," Adobe Stock, n.d., https://stock.adobe.com/images/maslow-s-hierarchy-of-needs-scalable-vector-illustration/141243251.

Author's note: The chart depicted incorporates this scalable vector as a component of the graphic. An emphasis graphic has been added on the left-hand side to illustrate the levels of belief (faith and grit) relative to Maslow's hierarchy. While Maslow initially proposed 5 levels of need, he later extended it to 8; however, these additional 3 levels can be encapsulated within the top 2 levels of the original 5.

55. Proverbs 29:18 (King James Version).

56. Nelson Mandela, https://www.goodreads.com/quotes/16243-education-is-the-most-powerful-weapon-which-you-can-use.

57. The full story of Joseph, his dad Jacob and their family can be found in the book of Genesis, chapters 27, 29-35, 37, 39-47.

58. According to the historical account in the Bible, a new name was given to Joseph by Pharaoh, the King Pharoah, which was the name Zaphenath-paneah meaning "God speaks, and he lives" or "revealer of secrets." This maybe one of the reasons why Joseph's brothers weren't aware of who he was when they met.

59. 2 Corinthians 13:5 (English Standard Version).

60. For those who are followers of Jesus, this scripture is meant to validate your faith and trust in God as the source that fuels your faith and grit needed to *face the mountain.*

61. James 1:27 (New International Version) states, "Religion that God our Father accepts as pure and faultless is this: to look after orphans and widows in their distress and to keep oneself from being polluted by the world." This verse highlights the distinction between mere religious observance and living out a faith that aligns with God's perspective and desires for our lives. It reflects the idea that true faith seeks to understand and follow God's will, transcending human traditions and rituals.

62. When someone says they are a person of faith, such as myself, they are referring to their belief in God, not necessarily advocating a specific religion. They are expressing a personal perspective on their identity, where they are coming from, and possibly their aspiration for a deeper, Level 5 Belief.

63. See Matthew 19:26 (ESV), "But Jesus looked at them and said, 'With man this is impossible, but with God all things are possible.'"

64. Teddy Roosevelt, *The Man in the Arena: Citizenship in a Republic,* April 23, 1910. The full speech is available at https://www.theodoreroosevelt.org/content.aspx?page_id=22&club_id=991271&module_id=339364.

65. *Air*, directed by Ben Affleck (2023; Culver City, CA: Amazon Studios/Warner Bros.), Amazon Prime. The film stars Matt Damon as Sonny Vaccaro, Damian Delano Young as Jordan, and Ben Affleck as CEO Phil Knight.

66. Michael Jordan, https://www.brainyquote.com/quotes/michael_jordan_621259#:~:text=Michael%20Jordan%20Quotes&text=My%20job%20was%20to%20go,what%20I%20shouldn't%20do.

67. Paul L. Gustavson, *IMAGINE: The Surprising Truth About Hope and the 12 Powerful Ways to Invent the Future* (Fredericksburg, VA: LeadEdgePress, 2022).

68. Teddy Roosevelt, *The Man in the Arena*.

69. James 2:26 (King James Version).

70. "H530 - 'ĕmûnâ - Strong's Hebrew Lexicon (KJV)," Blue Letter Bible, n.d., https://www.blueletterbible.org/lexicon/h530/kjv/wlc/0-1/.

71. Dr. Menachem Kellner, "*Emunah: Biblical Faith*," My Jewish Learning, April 3, 2015, https://www.myjewishlearning.com/article/emunah-biblical-faith.

72. Teddy Roosevelt, *The Man in the Arena*.

73. *Gladiator*, directed by Ridley Scott (2000; Universal City, CA: DreamWorks Pictures/DreamWorks Distribution), Amazon Prime. The film stars Russell Crowe as Roman General Maximus Decimus Meridius, Joaquin Phoenix as Commodus, and Richard Harris as Marcus Aurelius.

74. Oscar Wilde, https://www.goodreads.com/quotes/361850-the-critic-has-to-educate-the-public-the-artist-has.

75. "Image 1 of Abraham Lincoln Papers: Series 3. General Correspondence. 1837-1897: Abraham Lincoln, [March 4, 1865] (Second Inaugural Address; Endorsed by Lincoln, April 10, 1865)," The Library of Congress, n.d., https://www.loc.gov/resource/mal.4361300/?st=text. Lincoln gave this speech in the final weeks of the Civil War, fourteen months after his Gettysburg Address, given on November 19, 1863.

76. Abraham Lincoln, https://www.goodreads.com/quotes/565665-i-am-not-bound-to-win-but-i-am-bound.

77. Ritchie Torres, https://www.brainyquote.com/quotes/ritchie_torres_1216228.

78. Nike's "*Just Do It*" slogan debuted in 1988. It is regarded as one of the most iconic and effective advertising taglines of the twentieth century.

79. Dave Cornell, *Cultivate Courage: Face Fear. Fulfill Dreams* (Chicago: Smiling Dog Design, 2018).

80. "Inaugural Address, January 20, 1961," John F. Kennedy Presidential Library and Museum, https://www.jfklibrary.org/archives/other-resources/john-f-kennedy-speeches/inaugural-address-19610120.

81. John F. Kennedy, "Address at Rice University on the Nation's Space Effort," John F. Kennedy Presidential Library and Museum, delivered September 12, 1962, at Rice University, https://www.jfklibrary.org/learn/about-jfk/historic-speeches/address-at-rice-university-on-the-nations-space-effort.

82. Taken from: "Remarks at the University of Kansas, March 18, 1968," John F. Kennedy Presidential Library and Museum, https://www.jfklibrary.org/learn/about-jfk/the-kennedy-family/robert-f-kennedy/robert-f-kennedy-speeches/remarks-at-the-university-of-kansas-march-18-1968.

83. James 4:2 (New King James Version), "You do not have because you do not ask."

84. Bud Greenspan, *Wilma*, (Signet Books, 1977).

85. Wilma Rudolph, https://www.brainyquote.com/quotes/wilma_rudolph_885272.

86. Nelson Mandela, *A Long Walk to Freedom: The Autobiography of Nelson Mandela* (Time Warner Books, 1995).

87. New York Times, *Transcript of Talk by Reagan on South Africa and Apartheid*, July 23, 1986, https://www.nytimes.com/1986/07/23/world/transcript-of-talk-by-reagan-on-south-africa-and-apartheid.html.

88. Nelson Mandela, https://www.goodreads.com/quotes/11504915-the-greatest-glory-in-living-lies-not-in-never-falling.

89. Oliver Goldsmith, *The Citizen of the World, Or, Letters From a Chinese Philosopher, Residing in London, to His Friends in the Country*, https://www.goodreads.com/quotes/14574-our-greatest-glory-is-not-in-never-falling-but-in.

90. Daniel H. Pink, *The Power of Regret: How Looking Backward Moves Us Forward* (Penguin, 2022), 86.

91. Pink, *The Power of Regret*, 101.

92. Pink, *The Power of Regret*, 115.

93. Pink, *The Power of Regret*, 133.

94. Spurgeon Books, Posted on X by @SpurgeonBooks, July 31, 2023.

95. Philippians 4:8b (English Standard Version), "Excellence brings glory to God!"

96. Ephesians 6:10 (New Living Translation), "Be strong in the Lord and in his mighty power." Ephesians 6:11 (New International Version) says we should "take our stand" dressed in God's armor. Philippians 3:13-14 (NIV) tells us to "Forget what is behind and strain toward what is ahead. Press on toward the goal to win the prize."

97. *Miracle*, directed by Gavin O'Connor (2004; Burbank, CA: Pop Pop Productions/Buena Vista Pictures), Amazon Prime. This film, starring Kurt Russell as Coach Herb Brooks, depicts the story of how the 1980 Winter Olympics U.S. Men's Hockey Team defeated the Soviet Union's team of professionals. Released twenty-four years after it happened, it recreates that historic "Miracle on Ice" event.

98. Genesis 1:1 (NIV).

99. Genesis 1:26-31 (King James Version).

100. Psalm 121:1-2 (NIV).

101. Movieclips, "*Forrest Gump* (1994) - Run, Forrest, Run! Scene | Movieclips," February 15, 2023, https://www.youtube.com/watch?v=bSMxl1V8FSg.

102. Hebrews 11:1 (ESV).

103. Jim Rohn, https://quotefancy.com/quote/758460/Jim-Rohn-Asking-is-the-beginning-of-receiving-Make-sure-you-don-t-go-to-the-ocean-with-a.

104. Shakti Gawain, https://www.goodreads.com/quotes/183209-you-create-your-opportunities-by-asking-for-them.

105. Joel A. Barker, https://allauthor.com/quotes/8213/.

106. Bryant McGill, https://www.goodreads.com/quotes/663075-curiosity-is-one-of-the-great-secrets-of-happiness.

107. Walt Disney, https://www.brainyquote.com/quotes/walt_disney_132637.

108. Tim Brown, "*Some design principles,*" November 2009, https://designthinking.ideo.com/blog/some-design-principles.

109. Paul Gustavson, *Leaders Press On* (Fredericksburg, VA: Lead Edge Press, 2016). In this book, I share the story of Red McDaniel. I also recommend Red's biography, *Scars and Stripes*.

110. Eugene Red McDaniel, *Scars and Stripes: The True Story of One Man's Courage Facing Death as a POW in Vietnam* (Midpoint Trade Books), 27.

111. Red McDaniel, https://www.goodreads.com/ quotes/7119940-courage-is-not-the-absence-of-fear-it-s-the-presence-of.

112. McDaniel, *Scars and Stripes,* 137.

113. Victor Hugo, https://www.goodreads.com/quotes/42667-people-do-not-lack-strength-they-lack-will.

114. McDaniel, *Scars and Stripes,* 138.

115. McDaniel, *Scars and Stripes,* 138.

116. McDaniel, *Scars and Stripes,* 140.
Here's the excerpt of what Red shares:
"I knew what the apostle Paul meant when he said, 'Who shall separate us from the love of Christ? Shall tribulation, or distress, or persecution, or famine, or nakedness, or peril, or sword?' These things are very real to me now. And Paul answers, 'For I am persuaded that neither death, nor life, nor angels, nor principalities, nor powers, nor things present, nor things to come, nor height, nor depth, nor any other creature, shall be able to separate us from the love of God, which is in Christ Jesus our Lord' (Romans 8:35, 38-39)."

117. Marriot Key Card, 2011.

118. RetroStatic, "Sure 'Raise Your Hand if You're Sure' Deodorant Commercial (1985)," February 29, 2016, https://www.youtube. com/watch?v=oih0oB0m8uI. The Sure commercial aired frequently on television beginning in the mid-1980s.

119. Vince Lombardi allegedly told kick returner Travis Williams after he celebrated a touchdown in 1967, *"Travis, the next time you make it to the end zone, act like you've been there before."* Dan Evon, "FACT CHECK: What Football Coach Said 'Act Like You've Been There Before'?" Snopes, July 27, 2017, https://www.snopes. com/fact-check/act-like-youve-been-there-before/.

120. Joshua 1:5-66 (New Living Testament); emphasis mine.

121. Joshua 1:7 (NLT).

122. Joshua 1:9 (NLT).

123. Joshua 1:11 (NLT).

124. Joshua 1:16 (NLT).

125. Angeles Arrien, *The Second Half of Life: Opening the Eight Gates of Wisdom* (ed. 2010), https://libquotes.com/angeles-arrien.

126. 2 Corinthians 4:8-9 (NIV); emphasis mine.

127. Here are a few stats: 110 results in the New King James Version (NKJV), 138 results in the New International Version (NIV), 190 results in the New Living Testament (NLT).

128. Genesis 22:8 (NLT).

129. Deuteronomy 3:22 (NLT).

130. Deuteronomy 15:10 (NIV).

131. Joshua 1:9 (NIV).

132. Joshua 8:7 (NKJV).

133. Psalm 49:15 (NIV).

134. Psalm 59:10 (NLT).

135. Isaiah 50:9 (NKJV).

136. Micah 7:7 (NIV).

137. Zephaniah 2:7 (NKJV).

138. Matthew 10:19 (NLT).

139. Luke 1:37 (NLT).

140. Luke 14:14 (NLT).

141. John 14:13-14 (NLT). To quantify this promise, be mindful of James 4:3 (NLT), which says, *"And even when you ask, you don't get it because your motives are all wrong."*

142. Colossians 4:3 (NLT).

143. Philippians 4:19 (NIV).

144. Philemon 1:22 (NLT).

145. Revelation 21:4 (NKJV).

146. Proverbs 2:2-4 (NLT).

147. Matthew 7:7-8 (NLT).

148. FBC Laurens, in a blog titled *"Fear and Obedience,"* Joshua 1:1-9, dated September 30, 2012, the author shares the following. "Clearly, there are certainly moments in this text where Joshua seems at peace and calm. After all, Joshua is sure of God's presence. Likewise, Joshua, like no other Israelite, appears confident that God will give him and his people the tools and abilities they will need to conquer the Promise Land." Link no longer available. The most direct reference to Joshua and calm is found in *The New Unger's Bible Dictionary* online, (https://ia601208.us.archive.org/35/items/ ChristianE-booksIi/TheNewUngersBibleDictionary.pdf). Bottom of page 985, in the Character section, lines 6 and 10.

149. Philippians 4:13 (New King James Version).

150. Sterling Spellman, "Sometimes We Just Need a Gut Check!" December 14, 2016, https://www.linkedin.com/pulse/sometimes-we-just-need-gut-check-sterling-spellman/.

151. Marianne Williamson, https://quotefancy.com/quote/860721/Marianne-Williamson-Every-decision-you-make-reflects-your-evaluation-of-who-you-are.

152. Alison Levine, *On the Edge: Leadership Lessons from Mount Everest and Other Extreme Environments* (New York: Grand Central Publishing, 2014), 87.

153. Levine, *On the Edge,* 53.

154. 1 Samuel 17 (New International Version).

155. Malcom Gladwell, *David and Goliath: Underdogs, Misfits, and the Art of Battling Giants* (New York: Little, Brown and Company, 2013).

156. Matthew 8:26 (NIV).

157. These are proposed words; conjecture based on what Jesus might say. One scripture verse that provides a cross reference is John 16:33.

158. Northwestern Medicine, "*5 Things You Never Knew about Fear: Understanding the Science of Fear,*" https://www.nm.org/healthbeat/healthy-tips/emotional-health/5-things-you-never-knew-about-fear.

159. Newport Academy Staff, "How to Keep Calm and Carry On," *Newport Academy* (blog), November 22, 2022, https://www.newportacademy.com/resources/restoring-families/how-to-keep-calm.

160. Isaiah 43:18 (NIV) says, "Forget the former things; do not dwell on the past."

161. 1 Peter 5:7 (NIV).

162. Matthew 6:27 (NIV).

163. *Joe Montana: Cool Under Pressure* (2022; NFL Films), Season 1, Episode 5, "Crossroads," released January 27, 2022, on Peacock.

164. Bob Burg, *Adversaries Into Allies: Win People Over Without Manipulation or Coercion* (Portfolio, 2013). Burg coined the idea of "Let Calm Be Your Default" in this groundbreaking book. I highly recommend it.

165. "Calm is contagious" is a term commonly attributed to Rorke Denver, speaker and former U.S. Navy Seal. "Calm Is Contagious," 2024, https://now.leadercast.com/programs/calm-is-contagious.

166. Zig Ziglar, https://www.goodreads.com/quotes/1177933-you-can-have-everything-in-life-you-want-if-you.

167. Hoyt, Devoted, 87.

168. Team Hoyt's Story, *Team Hoyt. YES YOU CAN!* https://www.hoytrunningchairs.com/team-hoyts-story/.

169. Hoyt, *Devoted*, 198.

170. Rick Hoyt, "What My Father Means to Me," *Men's Health Magazine*, June 2010, https://www.menshealth.com/trending-news/a19518492/fatherhood-and-a-childs-disability.

171. U2, "I Still Haven't Found What I'm Looking For," track 2 on *The Joshua Tree.* Written by Paul David Hewson, Adam Clayton, Larry Mullen, Dave Evans. Island Records, 1987, album.

172. Greg Garrett, *We Get to Carry Each Other: The Gospel According to U2*, (Westminster John Knox Press), 9-10.

173. Bono, *Surrender* (New York: Knopf Doubleday Publishing Group, 2022), 508.

174. Bono, *Surrender*, 137.

175. Bono, *Surrender*, 136.

176. Matthew 23 (New International Version). In this passage, Jesus warns religious leaders against hypocrisy—projecting high morals but failing to live them out. He condemns their arrogance and focus on appearances over true righteousness. His call is for integrity, humility, and choosing faith over religion, emphasizing justice, mercy, and genuine devotion to God.

177. 1 Peter 2:1 (NIV).

178. Bono, *Surrender*, 145.

179. Refer back to the discussion in Chapter 5 about the distinction between faith and religion. This is not an argument against the church; rather, it highlights the prevalent challenge of hypocrisy that can arise. The focus here is to emphasize why understanding this difference is important for genuine connection and growth.

180. Bono. *Surrender*, 509.

181. John 10:10.

182. John 14:15-31.

183. Psalm 23 (New Century Version).

184. I encourage you to read Louis Giglio's book, *Don't Give the Enemy a Seat at Your Table: It's Time to Win the Battle of Your Mind* (Thomas Nelson, 2021).

185. Psalm 23:5-6.

186. John 3:16 (NCV). "God loved the world so much that he gave his one and only Son so that whoever believes in him may not be lost, but have eternal life."

1 John 3:16 (NCV). "This is how we know what real love is: Jesus gave his life for us. So we should give our lives for our brothers and sisters."

187. Luke 15:4-7 / Matthew 18:10-14. The parable of the lost sheep tells the story of a man who, upon losing one of his 100 sheep, leaves the 99 to search for the lost one until he finds it. When he does, he carries it home and celebrates with friends and neighbors. The parable emphasizes that everyone is valuable in God's eyes, and regardless of our past.

188. Philippians 2:6-11

189. Philippians 2:1-4

190. Micah 6:8 (NIV). "He has shown you, O mortal, what is good. And what does the Lord require of you? To act justly and to love mercy and to walk humbly with your God." This emphasizes walking with God, purpose, and living out responsibilities with humility and justice.

191. Galatians 6:2a (NIV). "Carry each other's burdens." This passage reflects the responsibility of honoring others by helping them along the way.

192. Joshua 1:5 (NIV).

193. Psalm 32:8 (NIV).

194. Isaiah 41:10 (NIV).

195. Jeremiah 29:11 (NIV).

196. 1 Thessalonians 2:4 (NIV). *"On the contrary, we speak as those approved by God to be entrusted with the gospel. We are not trying to please people but God, who tests our hearts."*

Authors Note: This verse highlights the responsibility and trust God places in us to share the message to others. focusing on pleasing Him rather than seeking human approval.

197. Genesis 1:28 (NIV). "God blessed them and said to them, 'Be fruitful and increase in number; fill the earth and subdue it. Rule over the fish in the sea and the birds in the sky and over every living creature that moves on the ground.'"

198. Matthew 25:14-30. The Parable of the Talents emphasizes the responsibility to use our gifts wisely.

199. 1 Peter 5:2a (NIV). "Be shepherds of God's flock that is under your care, watching over them—not because you must, but because you are willing."

200. Micah 6:8b (NIV). "And what does the Lord require of you? To act justly and to love mercy and to walk humbly with your God."

201. 2 Timothy 2:2 (NIV). "And the things you have heard me say in the presence of many witnesses entrust to reliable people who will also be qualified to teach others."

202. Mark 16:15 (NIV). "He said to them, 'Go into all the world and preach the gospel to all creation.'"

203. Galatians 6:2 (NIV).

204. 1 Corinthians 3:9 (NIV). The apostle Paul describes believers as "God's co-workers," indicating that God trusts us to work alongside Him on His mission.

205. Walt Disney, https://www.goodreads.com/quotes/27106-all-the-adversity-i-ve-had-in-my-life-all-my.

206. "Negative Thoughts and Brain Health | Amen Clinics," Sept. 16, 2020, https://www.amenclinics.com/blog/do-you-have-an-ant-infestation-in-your-head/.

207. Philippians 3:12-14. The apostle Paul talks about the importance of pressing on.

208. Pharisees were an ancient Jewish sect known for their strict adherence to Jewish Law and traditions. In the New Testament, they are often depicted as opponents of Jesus, criticized for their hypocrisy and legalism. They focused on outward religious observances while neglecting inner moral and spiritual values. Today, calling someone a "Pharisee" implies they are being hypocritical or overly concerned with the letter of the law rather than its spirit.

209. While our faith might be focused on a relationship with God (Level 5), it can be easy to judge ourselves and others based on the religious actions expected of us, like rules and regulations. This is where we can fall into the trap of religiosity.

210. Steve Jobs, https://www.goodreads.com/quotes/622900-my-model-for-business-is-the-beatles-they-were-four.

211. Charlie "Tremendous" Jones, https://www.goodreads.com/quotes/48905-you-will-be-the-same-person-in-five-years-as.

212. Psalm 23:4 (English Standard Version).

213. Martin Luther, https://www.goodreads.com/quotes/3182271-faith-is-a-living-daring-confidence-in-god-s-grace-so.

214. Philippians 2:5-11 (NIV) encourages us to have a similar mindset that Jesus had.

215. John 8:7 (NIV).

216. John 8:1-11 (New Living Translation).

217. Josh McDowell, https://www.goodreads.com/quotes/264719-rules-without-relationship-leads-to-rebellion.
Note: Religious bias, if it doesn't make you pious, can make you rebellious. Examine yourself. Are you a rebel? Has religion tripped you up, impacting your relationships? If so, what can you do to refocus on your relationships?

218. Regarding the sherpas who guided several of the leaders highlighted, here's a list I was able to compile:
Walt Disney: He would credit his colleague Ub Iwerks, his lead animator and co-creator of Mickey Mouse, as a sherpa. Ub helped him personally and professionally. Disney was private about his religious beliefs in public settings. However, he did have connections to Christian organizations and philanthropic endeavors, including contributing to the construction of the Christ the King statue in Rio de Janeiro, Brazil.
Bono: He credits his father, Bob Hewson, as well as Nelson Mandela and musicians such as Bob Dylan and David Bowie. Bono is vocal about his Christian faith and has credited Jesus and God as significant influences. In an interview with Ireland's national public broadcaster RTE, Bono said, *"I believe that Jesus was God and that he rose from the dead."*

219. Jack Kornfield, https://www.goodreads.com/quotes/41119-if-your-compassion-does-not-include-yourself-it-is-incomplete.

220. Billboard, https://www.pinterest.com/pin/spread-love-and-kindness-embracing-our-neighbors--16184879881797143/.

221. Fred Rogers, https://www.goodreads.com/quotes/7057503-all-of-us-at-some-time-or-other-need-help.

222. Bethany Hamilton, https://www.goodreads.com/quotes/1369127-i-ve-learned-life-is-a-lot-like-surfing-when-you.

223. *Soul Surfer,* directed by Sean McNamara (2011, Culver City, CA: TriStar Pictures), Amazon Prime. This film stars Anna Sophia Robb as Bethany Hamilton and Dennis Quaid as Tom Hamilton. See also Bethany Hamilton, https://www.quotes.net/mquote/1197652.

224. *Soul Surfer,* McNamara. See also Bethany Hamilton, https://www.quotes.net/mquote/1067269 and Bethany Hamilton, https://www.azquotes.com/quote/803155.

225. *The Tonight Show,* "Jeremy Renner on How His Near-Death Experience Changed His Outlook on Life (Extended)," YouTube, May 22, 2024, video, 10:44, https://www.youtube.com/watch?v=JN8E8HT3uiU.

226. *The Tonight Show*, "Jeremy Renner on His Near-Death Experience."

227. *CBS Mornings,* "Extended Cut: Jeremy Renner on Snowplow Accident, Advice for Younger Self and More," YouTube, May 22, 2024, video, 9:54, https://www.youtube.com/watch?v=5qiPE7x9-sU.

228. *The Tonight Show,* "Jeremy Renner on His Near-Death Experience."

229. We started our story list featuring Mister Rogers. His calling was to encourage us to be good neighbors. Being a good neighbor is being intentional with hope and serving others with honor. You can see that being intentional with hope is also important to Bethany Hamilton and Jeremy Renner. When it comes to Compassion, it's about consciously infusing possibility thinking into our daily lives and interactions, step by step.

230. Charles Spurgeon, https://www.brainyquote.com/quotes/charles_spurgeon_181483.

231. William Arthur Ward, ed., *For This One Hour* (Droke House, 1969).

232. Aristotle, https://www.brainyquote.com/quotes/aristotle_133079.

233. Jonas Salk, https://www.brainyquote.com/quotes/jonas_salk_389658.

234. See the Five Levels of Belief in chapter 4.

235. George Washington Carver, https://www.goodreads.com/quotes/11160811-where-there-is-no-vision-there-is-no-hope.

236. Eleanor Roosevelt, https://www.goodreads.com/quotes/845093-if-you-lose-money-you-lose-much-if-you-lose.

237. Jeremiah 29:11 (NIV).

238. Dalia Fahmy, "Key Findings About Americans' Belief in God," *Pew Research Center*, April 14, 2024, https://www.pewresearch.org/short-reads/2018/04/25/key-findings-about-americans-belief-in-god/.

239. The book of Isaiah within the Old Testament of the Bible shares about a Hope in the form of a coming Messiah who is identified as Emmanuel, which means "God is with Us." The Gospel of the New Testament is the account of Jesus, who fulfills the prophecy of the Messiah.

240. Plato, *The Republic, Book VI,* 509d-511e. For Plato, imagination represented a preliminary stage of reason in the pursuit of true knowledge.

241. Topical Bible: "Imagine," https://biblehub.com/topical/i/imagine.htm.

242. "Chashab Meaning - Hebrew Lexicon | Old Testament (NAS)," Bible Study Tools, https://www.biblestudytools.com/lexicons/hebrew/nas/chashab.html.

243. "Meditation," in the *International Standard Bible Encyclopedia Online,* https://www.internationalstandardbible.com/M/meditation.html.

244. "Meditation," in the *International Standard Bible Encyclopedia Online,* https://www.internationalstandardbible.com/M/meditation.html.

245. "*Meletao* Meaning - Greek Lexicon | New Testament (NAS)," Bible Study Tools, https://www.biblestudytools.com/lexicons/greek/nas/meletao.html.

246. Matthew 6:25-26 (New King James Version).

247. 1 Timothy 4:13, 15-16 (NKJV).

248. Hebrews 10:4 (New Living Translation).

249. Proverbs 23:7 (NKJV).

250. Romans 8:5 (NLT).

251. Philippians 4:8 (NLT).

252. 1 Chronicles 16:11-12 (New International Version).

253. Ephesians 3:20 (Contemporary English Version).

254 Colossians 3:2 (NLT).

255 Isaiah 65:17 (NLT).

256. "Desire," from Google's English Dictionary, provided by Oxford Languages. The word *longing* is listed as a simile.

257. Napolean Hill, https://www.goodreads.com/quotes/246161-the-starting-point-of-all-achievement-is-desire-keep-this.

258. Saint Augustine, https://www.brainyquote.com/quotes/saint_augustine_148536.

259. C.S. Lewis, *"Letters to Malcolm: Chiefly on Prayer,"* Letter IV. In this book, Lewis describes prayer as "a form of request" while discussing the nature of prayer and its various aspects.

260. C. S. Lewis, https://www.goodreads.com/quotes/1005539-i-pray-because-i-can-t-help-myself-i-pray-because.

261. Psalm 32:6. King David wrote this while journeying through a tough season. Despite his challenges, he finds solace in faith. He ends this passage with a declaration in verse 7. *"You are a hiding-place for me; you preserve me from trouble; you surround me with glad cries of deliverance."* That's a healthy picture of faith. (Both verses, New Revised Standard Version, Anglicised.)

262. Two verses that capture David's sentiment of seeking God's help in the face of difficulties include:

Psalm 121:1-2 (New International Version): "I lift up my eyes to the mountains—where does my help come from? My help comes from the Lord, the Maker of heaven and earth." This verse reflects David looking toward the mountains and acknowledging that his help comes from the Lord. It illustrates his reliance on God during times of challenge.

Psalm 3:4 (NIV): "I call out to the Lord, and he answers me from his holy mountain." This verse shows David praying and God answering him, providing divine assistance during his struggles.

263. Brian Tracy, https://www.goodreads.com/quotes/881048-the-key-to-success-is-to-focus-our-conscious-mind.

264. Meister Eckhart, https://www.goodreads.com/quotes/644785-if-the-only-prayer-you-ever-say-in-your-entire.

265. Matthew 7:7-8.

266. Matthew 6:9-10 (New King James Version).

267. Matthew 6:11-12 (NKJV).

268. Matthew 6:13 (NKJV).

269. For more about the Reticular Activating System (RAS), see my book *IMAGINE* (Fredericksburg, VA: LeadEdgePress, 2022). Also, check out Mark Batterson's book, *The Circle Maker* (Grand Rapids, MI: Zondervan, 2016).

270. Sanjana Gupta, "9 Scientifically Proven Ways in Which Praying Is Actually Good for Your Health!" *Indiatimes*, May 6, 2016, https://www.indiatimes.com/health/healthyliving/9-ways-in-which-praying-is-actually-good-for-your-health-backed-by-science-245787.html.

271. Saint Augustine of Hippo, https://www.goodreads.com/quotes/377812-pray-as-though-everything-depends-on-god-and-work-as.

272. Philippians 4:6-7a (NLT). In verse 7, the apostle Paul adds, "His peace will guard your hearts and minds as you live in Christ Jesus."

273. Philippians 4:8-9 (NIV).

274. James 1:6 (Good News Translation).

275. Ephesians 3:20 (New International Revised Version).

276. Jeremiah 29:11 (NIV).

277. Ed DeCosta, Catalyst Associates. Unfortunately, Ed's list is unavailable online presently. The resource I received from him was a handout at a conference in 2012.

278. Marian Wright Edelman, https://www.goodreads.com/quotes/3342-you-really-can-change-the-world-if-you-care-enough.

279. Catherine Duncan, "Prayer," Taking Charge of Your Wellbeing, https://www.takingcharge.csh.umn.edu/prayer. Look for the heading, "Is there evidence for benefits of prayer?"

280. The quote, *"Practice like you'll play because you'll play like you practiced,"* is of anonymous origin but is widely attributed to various sports figures, including coaches and athletes. A related term used in the military is *"Train like you fight,"* which is a principle that encourages training in conditions that replicate the stress of combat.

281. Suzy Kassem, https://quotefancy.com/quote/431143/Suzy-Kassem-Doubt-kills-more-dreams-than-failure-ever-will.

282. There are too many verses to list in the confines of this book to highlight the consequences of improper imagination. Discover more at http://theimaginebook.com.

283. Mark 11:22-23 (New International Version).

284. Mark 11:24 (NIV).

285. James 1:6 (NIV).

286. James 1:8 (NIV).

287. Mark 9:23 (New Living Translation).

288. Zig Ziglar, https://www.goodreads.com/quotes/915549-always-remember-that-your-present-situation-is-not-your-final.

289. Jim Rohn, https://www.goodreads.com/quotes/28439-discipline-is-the-bridge-between-goals-and-accomplishment.

290. Proverbs 3:11-12 (NIV).

291. James 1:2-4 (NIV).

292. James 1:5 (NIV).

293. Proverbs 3:13-14 (NIV).

294. Iyanla Vanzant, https://www.goodreads.com/quotes/4491463-comparison-is-an-act-of-violence-against-the-self-it. Vanzant is an American inspirational speaker, lawyer, spiritual teacher, author, and television personality.

295. Luke 12:22-23 (NIV).

296. Luke 12:24-26, 28 (NIV).

297. Founders Online, https://founders.archives.gov/documents/Franklin/01-03-02-0105#BNFN-01-03-02-0105-fn-0004. See IX., under January 12, 1748.

298. Steven Curtis Chapman, "Declaration of Dependence," track 10 on *Declaration*, Sparrow Records, 2001, compact disc.

299. Stephen Curtis Chapman, https://www.lyrics.com/lyric/14050306/Steven+Curtis+Chapman/Declaration+of+Dependence.

300. Matthew 7:7-8.

301. Romans 12:2 (NIV).

302. Proverbs 23:7 (New King James Version).

303. Albert Einstein, https://www.goodreads.com/quotes/1799-the-world-as-we-have-created-it-is-a-process.

304. Earl Nightingale, https://www.goodreads.com/quotes/990479-we-become-what-we-think-about.

305. Craig Groeschel, https://www.goodreads.com/work/quotes/87129574-winning-the-war-in-your-mind-change-your-thinking-change-your-life.

306. Muhammad Ali, https://www.goodreads.com/quotes/96639-what-you-re-thinking-is-what-you-re-becoming.

307. The "Anyway" poem, often associated with Mother Teresa, was actually written by Dr. Kent M. Keith. His original version is known as "The Paradoxical Commandments."
"Anyway | Paradoxical Commandments," ParadoxicalComm, 1968, https://www.paradoxicalcommandments.com/. Mother Teresa had a version of this poem on the wall of her home for children in Calcutta.

308. All Saints Catholic Church, https://allsaints.cc/documents/2020/5/Mother%20Teresa%20_anyway_%20quotes%202020.pdf.

309. Teddy Roosevelt, *The Man in the Arena: Citizenship in a Republic,* April 23, 1910. The full speech is available at https://www.theodoreroosevelt.org/content.aspx?page_id=22&club_id=991271&module_id=339364.

310. Sir Edmund Hillary, https://www.azquotes.com/quote/840677.

311. *Invictus,* directed by Clint Eastwood (2009; Burbank, CA: Warner Bros.), Amazon Prime.

312. William Ernest Henley. Academy of American Poets, "Invictus," Poets.org, 1893, https://poets.org/poem/invictus?gad_source=1&gclid=CjwKCAjwlbu2BhA3EiwA3yXyu6jSm0l0Qby_TN9PMizrp52A-xeK1clBgwLogZ9clh0jDOw1jCQpihoCw8sQAvD_BwE.

313. In my research, I found this incredible story from the words of Pienaar, the rugby team captain. The article is titled, "South Africa's real 'Invictus' rugby captain recalls 'special' relationship with Mandela." He shares about the profound impact of Mandela, and the kindness and grace he offered, as well as the way he led. Here's the link: https://www.nbcnews.com/news/world/south-africas-real-invictus-rugby-captain-recalls-special-relationship-mandela-flna2d11703188.

314. Shosholoza, https://mudcat.org/thread.cfm?threadid=36657.

315. Shosholoza – Traditional song from Zimbabwe, https://heatherhoustonmusic.com/song/shosholoza/.

316. Kevin Hall, *Aspire*, (New York: HarperCollins, 2009), Foreword.

317. Secretary-General's remarks at unveiling of Nelson Mandela statue [as delivered], 24 September 2018, https://www.un.org/sg/en/content/sg/statement/2018-09-24/secretary-generals-remarks-unveiling-of-nelson-mandela-statue-delivered.

318. Mark Batterson, *Draw the Circle: The 40 Day Prayer Challenge* (Grand Rapids, MI: Zondervan, 2018), Day 14 – Speak to the Mountain.

319. Matthew 17:19-21 (New Century Version).

320. Jeremy Renner, Facebook Stories, posted February 22, 2024, https://www.facebook.com/JeremyRennerOfficial.
Renner's social media expresses the idea that obstacles, problems, and failures, rather than being mere setbacks, actually contribute to the foundation of success. Renner suggests that these challenges are not enemies but rather allies that help build the strength and resilience necessary for achievement. He also offers encouragement to those who struggle, emphasizing the power of belief and collective effort in overcoming difficulties and achieving great things, metaphorically "moving mountains." He suggests that people can overcome even the most daunting challenges.

321. John 16:33 (The Living Bible).

LEAD EDGE PRESS BOOKS

Books by PAUL GUSTAVSON

FACE THE MOUNTAIN:
Discovering Resilience and
the Power to Change the World

IMAGINE:
The Suprising Truth About Hope and
The 12 Powerful Ways to Invent the Future

BREAKING AVERAGE:
The Seven Critical Factors to
Team Strong Leadership

SPEECH BLUEPRINT:
Using Simon Sinek's TED Talk
as a Model to "Inspire Action"

LEADERS PRESS ON:
Discovering the Power of Perseverance

Books by BARBARA VALENTINE GUSTAVSON

PERMISSION TO BE BOLD:
A Guide to Loving Yourself, Living Fully,
and Leaving Your Mark in the World

Lead Edge
PRESS

Previous Praise for IMAGINE

"*IMAGINE* offers a fresh approach to leading from the inside out. Its combination of science and stories will spark new ideas—and open your eyes to the hidden possibilities around us."

— **Daniel H. Pink**
#1 New York Times bestselling author of
The Power of Regret, Drive, and *To Sell Is Human*

"*IMAGINE* captures the essence of what it takes to be future minded yet situationally aware of the present. Both are critical to how you live and how you lead."

— **Mark Batterson**
New York Times bestselling author,
The Circle Maker

"Einstein called Imagination *"a preview of life's coming attractions."* He went on to add that it's *"more important than knowledge."* This book is a fresh take on how to make better use of it. I highly recommend it."

— **Dr. Daniel Amen, MD**
CEO and Founder, *Amen Clinics, BrainMD*, and
the *Change Your Brain, Change Your Life Foundation*

"*IMAGINE* offers a grand tour into the realm of imagination. Whether you're creating a vision for yourself or for your team, organization, family, community, or nation, let this invaluable resource be your guide."

— **Dr. Gloria J. Burgess**
Author, *Flawless Leadership,
Dare to Wear Your Soul on the Outside*, and *Pass It On!*

"Paul is a student of leadership and growing systems and people. In his newest book, this passion and commitment comes through with clarity and competence."

— **Kary Oberbrunner**
WSJ & USA Today bestselling author, and
CEO of *Igniting Souls*

Previous Praise for BREAKING AVERAGE

"*BREAKING AVERAGE* is a skillfully crafted, insightful resource for anyone who seeks to develop a high-performance team. Written from experience, wisdom, and a deep understanding of how leaders develop collaborative cultures, *Breaking Average* is approachable, refreshing, and empowering! It is filled with actionable tools that inspire and activate business success through team performance!"

— **Joseph Michelli**
Bestselling author,
The Airbnb Way, and *Driven to Delight*

"*BREAKING AVERAGE* offers a fresh perspective on what it takes to build a team. It's a difference maker. The Seven Critical Factors alone are invaluable. But this book goes even further. It offers relevant stories, practical tips, and tools to help score you and your team."

— **Bonnie St. John**
Bestselling author of *Micro-Resilience*,
Paralympic Medalist and CEO, *Blue Circle Leadership*

"Everyone knows that teamwork is essential to success. *BREAKING AVERAGE* provides practical guidelines for building above-average teams that will lead to above-average results."

— **Ken Davis**
Author, Speaker, Communication Coach

"Interesting stories and actionable ideas will help you create a successful team or lead the team you have more effectively. Break average by reading and using this book!"

— **Mark Sanborn**
New York Times best-selling author of *The Fred Factor*

www.ingramcontent.com/pod-product-compliance
Lightning Source LLC
Chambersburg PA
CBHW051824090426
42736CB00011B/1631